Table of Contents

S0-DZB-598

Premier hometown restaurants

Northern Indiana, Region 1

Western Indiana, Region 2

Eastern Indiana, Region 3

A wealth of Hoosier dining, travel adventure await users of this book

Use this book. We guarantee doing so will bring memorable dining experiences, new friends and enriching discoveries into your life.

Even some of us lifelong Hoosiers who were involved in the book's development have been astonished to learn of the many undiscovered Hoosier treasures in our hometown restaurants as well as the state's intriguing visitor attractions.

For instance, we learned—and you will, too, if you use this book—that Indiana's only Spanish restaurant is in Valparaiso and the only place to eat a Dubois Dookey sandwich is in Huntingburg at the Fourth Street Deli.

There is treasure, to be sure, in the culinary delights offered by the hundreds of Favorite Hometown Restaurants so proudly recommended by local officials. But, riches also exist in the wealth of museums, shopping and recreation attractions throughout Indiana.

We also hope you'll discover—as we have in our communications with the restaurants—that the folks who own and operate our hometown restaurants are among the most hospitable and cordial anywhere. Many, like this year's premier hometown restaurant, The Beef House near Covington, are family owned and operated.

We encourage you to tell us about your experiences using this guide. We'd like your suggestions for future editions, especially about any new favorite hometown restaurant discoveries.

Finally, we thank you. The purchase price of this book will help improve the quality of municipal government in Hoosier communities since all profits are dedicated to the training and education of local officials.

The IACT Editorial Staff

Good restaurants draw diners and dollars to local economy

For mayors and other municipal leaders, good restaurants represent more than a good meal. They are a valuable economic asset.

As Columbus Mayor Robert Stewart preaches to his colleagues, "If you don't have a good restaurant in your community, take steps to get one!" Considered one of the most successful mayors in the nation at bringing new industry to his All America City, Mayor Stewart observes that when a prospective new business leader comes site-scouting to your community, "where do you take him or her for a meal?" Stewart added, "If you must go to another city for a decent meal, that's where the new plant might go!"

Local officials also know that when a popular restaurant draws diners from outside the community it usually means additional shopping, lodging and other tourism dollars.

So, eat, drink and be mindful that your dining and tourist dollar is contributing to the economy of Hoosier communities.

What do Hoosiers like best to eat?

The answer would appear to be beef, since two of the three most popular restaurants nominated for this publication are steak houses. However, four of the "Top Ten" feature fried chicken as a top entree. Other dishes which dominated the recommendations included catfish, tenderloin sandwiches, pork chops, and Amish country cooking.

Central Indiana, Region 4

South Central Indiana, Region 5

Southern Indiana, Region 6

How to use this guide

On the following pages you will find listings of restaurants from nominations made by locally elected city and town officials. The listings are arranged by region and municipality. Included in the information for each listing are the restaurant's address, phone number and directions, where possible. We've also provided you with a summary highlighting favorite meals, specialties of the house, or a bit of history about each restaurant, along with hours of operation, dress, average meal cost, and accepted credit cards.

We hope the format and information are useful, and that you learn a little bit of history along the way. The following abbreviations or symbols are used throughout this guide:

Days of the week (under "open"):
Su, M, T, W, Th, F, S

Price code for average cost of entree:
❖ = under $5
❖❖ = $5-$10
❖❖❖ = $10-15
❖❖❖❖ = $15-$20
❖❖❖❖❖ = over $20

Credit card abbreviations:
MC = Master Card
V = Visa
AmEx = American Express
CB = Carte Blanche
Di = Discover
DC = Diners' Club

How the state is divided

The six regions used in this book have been established by the Indiana Department of Tourism. Many thanks to them for allowing us to use their maps.

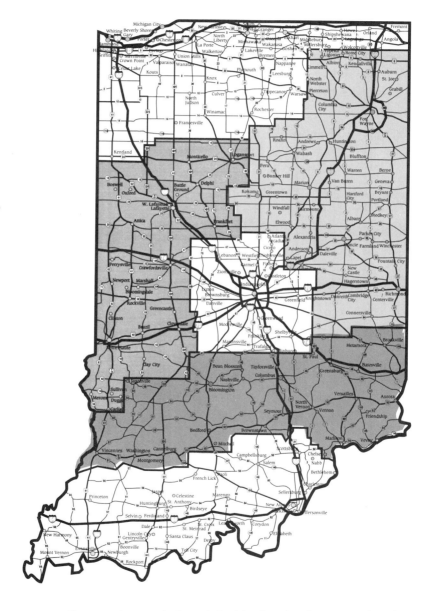

This map is for regional reference only. Not all roads and towns are indicated. Please consult a state highway map for complete travel information.

The Top Ten

*Indiana's number one Hometown Favorite
in Wright hands for primetime dining*

THE BEEF HOUSE, COVINGTON

The Beef House Restaurant, near Covington in scenic West Central Indiana, is a family owned-and-operated creative expression of Hoosier dining at its best. So, bring the family when you visit what municipal officials have designated as this year's premier hometown restaurant.

On arrival, you'll find a friendly greeting, probably from a member of the Wright family. As you enter, stop just inside the entrance to shop at the glass butcher's display case where several rows of juicy, high choice beefsteaks entice the newcomer. On the Wednesday evening our staff visited the restaurant four off-menu fresh seafood specials were offered.

The business has been in the Wright family hands since 1963, when it was founded by Warren and Ellen Wright. The late Mr. Wright decided to open a steak house after unusual success serving ribeyes cooked over a charcoal grill at a 4-H event. In 1967 son Bob and his wife, Bonnie, assumed management and began serving the restaurant's signature homemade Beef House yeast rolls and fresh jam. The rolls, made daily from scratch, are a delicacy Bob discovered while gaining a degree in restaurant management up the road at Purdue University.

Our test night server, Mary Anne Scott, has been happily employed with The Beef House for six years and likes it so well she doesn't mind the one hour and twenty-minute round-trip drive from her Lafayette home. Like Mary Anne, many of the Beef House personnel are long-term employees.

Beverage options include an enticing array of cocktails, beers (served in frosted mugs) and an extensive wine list. Our appetizer recommendations include the many fresh-made soups, especially the broccoli and chicken rice.

While many recent diners suggest the ribeye steaks as the restaurant's flagship fare, our visit reinforced reports from municipal officials who declare that the filet mignons are "the best." Indeed, three members of our tasting group endorsed the filets as "the best we've ever had—anywhere."

Prices are moderate to expensive, depending on your taste and capacity. Some samples from the menu include: 8 oz. rib eye steak, $12.50; filet mignon, $16.95; 20 oz. T-bone, $17.25; walleye pike, $14.25; petit filet mignon and crab legs, $25.25. All dinners include soup, salad bar or choice of salad, vegetable, rolls, butter and beverage. A special 11 a.m.

Located off I-74 Exit 4 on SR 63 (after exiting, look for the large "Beef House" sign on the northwest side of the intersection), about 4 miles west of Covington.

The Beef House nominators include: Phyllis Lambert, clerk-treasurer, Fairview Park; Mayor Dave Berkemeier, Tipton; Mayor Ken Crabb, Brazil; Newtown Councilmember Jim Robinson; and Clerk-Treasurer JoAnn Anderson and Councilmember Henry Schmitt, both of Covington.

to 3:30 p.m. Sunday menu offers pan fried chicken, roast pork, and roast beef and steak dishes at prices ranging from $10.25 to $12. The restaurant is open for breakfast and lunch and is closed only on Thanksgiving and Christmas days.

Reservations are accepted with the exception of Saturdays by calling (317) 793-3947.

Second Place
THE LOG INN, WARRENTON

The Log Inn is located a mile east of U.S. 41, just north of I-64, on Old State Rd., about 12 miles north of Evansville.

The Log Inn is believed to be the oldest restaurant in Indiana. Abraham Lincoln reportedly ate at the restored log coach stop and trading post in what is now called the Lincoln Room in 1844. If it was available then, he probably ordered the family-style fried chicken dinner—folks like Chandler Town Manager John Hillenbrand and Haubstadt Clerk-Treasurer Bonnie Wagner and several members of the Association of Cities and Towns staff swear there's none better anywhere. Lincoln would have been pleased to know that the cellar of the 170-year-old restaurant was once used as a hiding place for fleeing slaves. The action today, however, is upstairs where the family-style dinners come complete with all the trimmings. Call (812) 867-3216 for reservations. Open 4 to 10 p.m., The Log Inn is closed Sunday and Monday.

Third Place
ST. ELMO STEAK HOUSE, INDIANAPOLIS

St. Elmo is located at 127 South Illinois St. near the circle.

The most popular Indianapolis dining spot for visiting municipal officials is the venerable St. Elmo Steak House, where the decor reflects the age when the restaurant first opened in 1902. The walls are decorated with photographs of famous dinner guests at this award-winning eatery. Table service by tuxedo-clad servers is swift and efficient. Portage Mayor Sammie Maletta suggests the jumbo shrimp cocktail before a hefty steak. St. Elmo is open seven days a week. Hours are Monday-Saturday, 4-10:30 p.m., and Sunday, 5-9:30 p.m. Reservations are recommended by calling (317) 635-0636.

Fourth Place
THE STORY INN, STORY

The Story Inn is located about 14 miles south of Nashville on SR 135.

Enjoy the tranquil Brown County scenery surrounding The Story Inn. Because they are usually booked well in advance, reservations are a must; call (812) 988-2273. White linen dining in this popular restaurant and inn is enhanced by the antique-lined walls, ancient potbellied stove and, in warm weather, the back porch, all pleasantly placed in a former general store. Owners Gretchen and Bob Haddix are most proud of the beef Wellington. The turtle cheese cake is a legendary favorite.

MILLER'S FISH SUPPERS, COLFAX

A favorite of visitors on their way to Purdue University events, Miller's is deservedly famous for their catfish suppers. The Miller family also brags about the broasted chicken and such recent broiled menu items as halibut and stuffed shrimp. Miller's is open from 4-10 p.m. Tuesday-Saturday, and is closed on Sunday, Monday and most holidays. The restaurant does not accept reservations. For more information, call Manager Mike Miller, (317) 324-2656.

Miller's is located just off U.S. 52 between Lafayette and Indianapolis.

Sixth Place
GIOVANNI'S, MUNSTER

Giovanni's is the most popular Italian Restaurant among local officials. Favorite dishes among regional folks, including Munster Town Manager Tom DeGiulio, are the veal picata and chicken vesuvio. Be sure, however, to save room for the pride of owner Nancy LoDuca—the Grand Marnier mousse cake. Ask about Chef Tim Merkle's daily lunch and dinner specials. Closed Sunday, Giovanni's hours are 11 a.m.-11 p.m. Monday-Friday, and 5 p.m.-midnight Saturday. Reservations are a must on Fridays and Saturdays; call (219) 836-6220.

Giovanni's is located at 603 Ridge Rd. (U.S. 6) in Munster.

Seventh Place
THE GASTHOF AMISH RESTAURANT AND VILLAGE, MONTGOMERY

A dining and cultural experience awaits visitors to The Gasthof in Montgomery. Built with Indiana oak and poplar by Amish carpenters, the large restaurant features fried chicken and roast beef. Closed Sunday, the complex also includes a craft and gift shop. On Tuesdays and Wednesdays from May-October visit the 100-booth outdoor flea market. Guided tours presenting the Amish way of life also may be scheduled. The Gasthof is open 11 a.m.-8 p.m., Monday-Friday, and 8 a.m.-9 p.m., Saturday. For reservations call (812) 486-3977.

The Gasthof is just north of U.S. 50/150 between Washington and Loogootee.

Eighth Place
WELLIVER'S, HAGERSTOWN

Approaching a half-century of culinary service to diners from across the nation, Welliver's provides a virtual harvest smorgasbord of fine foods. Opened in 1946, specialities include skillet fried country chicken, steamed shrimp and homemade cinnamon bread. Open only for dinner Thursday-Sunday. Ask about special prices for children and seniors. Telephone: (317) 489-4131.

You'll find Welliver's at 40 E. Main St.

A Different
Drummer at the
Walden Inn is near
the DePauw
University campus
in the historic
downtown
Greencastle
square.

A DIFFERENT DRUMMER, WALDEN INN, GREENCASTLE

You may be greeted by Dublin-born Innkeeper/Chef Matt O'Neill at this award-winning restaurant and inn, enhanced by Amish-crafted furniture, a lobby library with fireplace and classic Americana decor. The restaurant features homemade breads and pastries along with a sumptuous beef wellington. Ask for Chef O'Neill's daily special. Open seven days for breakfast, lunch and dinner, reservations are encouraged; call (317) 653-2761.

Tenth Place
DAS DUTCHMAN ESSENHAUS AMISH COUNTRY KITCHEN, MIDDLEBURY

Das Dutchman
Essenhaus Amish
Country Kitchen is
west of Middlebury
on U.S. 20.

Amish cooking and all-you-can-eat dining are only part of the "Essenhaus experience," which also includes lodging and shopping opportunities according to Middlebury Town Manager Marcel Coulomb. An Amish bakery offers such delicacies as homemade noodles. Closed Sunday, The Amish Country Kitchen is open 6 a.m.-8 p.m. Monday-Thursday, and 6 a.m.-9 p.m. Friday-Saturday. Call for reservations: (219) 825-9471.

Honorable Mention:
(information about these restaurants appears in the regional descriptions)

Amish Acres Restaurant, Nappanee
Beach Cafe, Gary
Company's Coming, Scottsburg
Country Lounge, Hobart
The Country Inn, Topeka
Gray Brothers Cafeteria, Mooresville
Koch's Brau Haus, Oldenburg
Olympia Candy Kitchen, Goshen
Red Geranium, New Harmony
Stoll's Country Inn, Linton
The Strongbow Inn, Valparaiso
Weinantz Food & Spirits, Columbus
Whisky's, Lawrenceburg

Northern Indiana provides pinnacle of touring pleasure

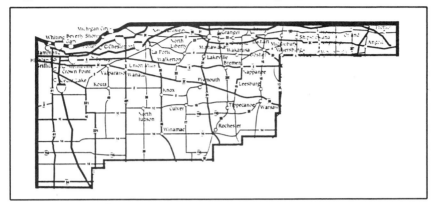

The alluring charm of Amish country, the delightful outdoor diversions offered by Lake Michigan's shoreline and the cultural attractions of one of Indiana's most urbanized areas provide the pinnacle of pleasure for the northbound traveler.

A good starting point for exploring the Indiana Dunes is the Paul H. Douglas Environmental Center on Lake Street in Gary, where interactive exhibits introduce visitors to the area once described by poet Carl Sandburg as "A signature of time and eternity every bit as moving as the Grand Canyon or Yosemite National Park."

Numerous marinas at Hammond, East Chicago and Michigan City offer charter boat fishing for coho, Chinook salmon and trout.

Top-name entertainment, fine dining, a comedy club, and superior lodging are available in Merrillville at the Radisson Star Plaza.

While in the Lake County seat of Crown Point, we suggest a visit to the historic courthouse which features 13 shops and a museum. Built in 1878, previous local officials there provided marriage licenses to such romantics as Rudolph Valentino, Muhammad Ali and Ronald Reagan.

A little farther south, in Cedar Lake, rediscover the lost art of ice cutting at the Lake of the Red Cedars Museum, built in 1865, where fascinating displays include the tools of the ancient ice-cutting industry and those of native son, world-famous podiatrist and shoemaker Dr. William Scholl.

For a restful interlude in Valparaiso, home of popcorn king Orville Redenbacher, visit the Valparaiso University campus Chapel of the Resurrection, the largest university chapel in the world. If you have a taste for the grape, drop by Valpo's Anderson's Orchard and Winery.

The golden dome of the

5

University of Notre Dame marks the center of pinnacle country and should be at the top of your itinerary. Call (219) 631-5726 for information on walking tours of the 150-year-old campus, including stops at the Snite Museum of Art and the Shrine of the Grotto of Our Lady of Lourdes, built in 1896. For decades, another top institution in South Bend was the Studebaker Motor Car Company. A modern museum containing the first and last car built by the firm offers a glimpse of past automotive glory.

In the hidden gem category, visit the Midwest Museum of American Art in downtown Elkhart which contains a collection of Ansel Adams photographs and what is believed to be the largest collection of Norman Rockwell lithographs anywhere.

Goshen's shopping opportunities include the 1890's Old Bag Factory with 17 studios and craft shops.

A "must see" stop is Amish Acres on U.S. 6 in Nappanee for a unique and educational experience.

No Indiana Amish Country tour is complete without a stop in Shipshewana, where a multimedia presentation at Menno-Hof on the Amish and Mennonite way of life will give added significance to your visit. A shopper's delight awaits visitors on Tuesdays and Wednesdays, May through October, at the world-famous Shipshewana Auction and Flea Market.

Sunday's are special May through October in Culver; that's when the Culver Military Academy parades its Black Horse Troop of skilled riders in full military dress.

At the Fulton County Museum near Rochester you can obtain a map for a self-guided tour of the area's picturesque round barns which were popular at the turn of the century.

There's much more to do at the top of Indiana. For more information, call the following local visitor centers:

Elkhart County...(219) 872-5055
Fulton County..(219) 223-6773
Jasper County..(219) 866-8223
Knox..(219) 772-5548
Kosciusko County.................................1-800-800-6090
LaGrange County....................................(219) 463-8090
Lake County................(219) 980-1617 or 1-800-ALL-LAKE
LaPorte County..1-800-634-2650
Marshall County..........(219) 936-9000 or 1-800-626-5353
Newton County..(219) 474-5177
Porter County.............(219) 926-2255 or 1-800-283-TOUR
South Bend/Mishawaka...
..................................(219) 289-0358 or 1-800-882-7881
Steuben County..........(219) 665-5386 or 1-800-LAKE-101

ANGOLA

The Hatchery

118 South Elizabeth Street
Angola, IN 46703
(219) 665-9957

The hatchery got its name because the dining room was a chicken hatchery in the 50s and 60s.

Dubbed "one of the best kept secrets" in Steuben County, The Hatchery offers diners everything from fresh seafood to tantalizing steaks. Both the filet Alaska and the sauteed soft shell crab (in season) are highly recommended. A pianist entertains diners on weekends. Reservations advised.

Open: 5-9 p.m. M-Th, 5-10 p.m. F-S, closed Su, holidays
Dress: casual/dressy   ❖❖❖❖   MC V AmEx CB DC

CEDAR LAKE

restaurant nominated by Geraldine H. Kortokrax, clerk-treasurer

The Bread Basket

13951 Huseman Street
Cedar Lake, IN 46303
(219) 374-4661

A charming family-owned eatery with an antique decor is what you'll find at The Bread Basket. All of the food is home-cooked and delicious; the thin Swedish hot croissant is the restaurant's most popular item. Clerk-Treasurer Kortokrax recommends the open reuben and homemade soup. Sorry, no reservations.

Open: 10 a.m.-4 p.m. T-S, closed Su-M
Dress: casual   ❖

restaurant nominated by Robert Carnahan, former councilmember

Donelli's Pizza

9707 West 133 Avenue
P.O. Box 466
Cedar Lake, IN 46303

When the town council meetings run late into the evening and municipal appetites grow ravenous, Donelli's Pizza is what overworked councilmembers order to appease their hunger. Delivery and carry out available. Sorry, no reservations.

Open: 3-11 p.m. M-Th, 3-midnight F-S, 2-11 p.m. Su
Dress: very casual   ❖❖

7

CHESTERTON

restaurants nominated by Robert E. Crone, councilmember

Duneland Pizza

520 Broadway
Chesterton, IN 46304
(219) 926-1163

In Chesterton, if it's pizza you crave, head for Duneland Pizza where you'll find five styles of pizza and 15 different toppings to tempt your tastebuds. The "supreme pizza" gets rave reviews— but after nearly a quarter-century in operation, they've perfected all of their pizzas. You also can get fantastic sandwiches, lasagna and spaghetti. Sorry, no reservations.
Open: 4-10 p.m. Su-Th, 4-11 p.m. F-S
Dress: very casual   ❖   **MC V AmEx Di DC**

The Port Drive-In

419 North Calumet Road
Chesterton, IN 46304
(219) 926-3500

Take Chesterton Exit off I-94, go south to Indian Boundary Road (first light), and turn right.

For a good time and the best chili dogs in the Midwest, glide on into the Port where the carhops zip about on roller skates. Or, if you prefer to dine indoors, enjoy the photos of employees who have worked at the Port during the last 30 years. Call ahead; the Port Drive-In is seasonally operated. Sorry, no reservations.
Open: 11 a.m.-10 p.m. daily
Dress: very casual   ❖

CROWN POINT

restaurant nominated by Robert Kerr, councilmember

Twelve Islands

114 South Main Street
Crown Point, IN 46307
(219) 663-5070

Look for the famous county courthouse, Twelve Islands is on the east side.

Greek specialties are mingled with many American favorites on the menu at Twelve Islands. You're sure to find something delicious. Among the most popular offerings: Angelo's salad and the Greek salad. Reservations accepted.
Open: 8 a.m.-9 p.m. M-S, 8 a.m.-7 p.m. Su
Dress: very casual   ❖   **MC V**

restaurants nominated by Bobetta Washburn, clerk-treasurer

Cafe Max

113 South Main Street
Culver, IN 46511
(219) 842-2511

From the minute you enter this former movie house, it's obvious Cafe Max is a local favorite. Memorabilia of the town, lake and Culver Academy grace the walls. The homemade bread, soups and omelettes come highly recommended. The sinful French toast and fresh-baked cinnamon roll served French toast style are popular, too. Sorry, no reservations.

Open: 6 a.m.-2 p.m. daily
Dress: very casual ❖

Pinder's Restaurant

530 Ohio Street
Culver, IN 46511
(219) 842-3415

If it's not made on-site, it doesn't belong at Pinder's Restaurant according to Clerk-Treasurer Washburn. All food is prepared by a Pinder family member, including the homemade pies. A wide range of selections, an outstanding Sunday buffet and reasonable prices are features at this family dining favorite. Reservations accepted.

Open: 4-8 p.m. T-Th, 4-9 p.m. F-S, 11 a.m.-3 p.m. Su, closed M
Dress: casual ❖❖ MC V

restaurant nominated by Ellen Krulewitch, councilmember

Lucchese' Deli

205 East Jackson Boulevard
Elkhart, IN 46516
(219) 522-4137

Homemade bread and pasta highlight the menu at Lucchese' Deli, where you'll find large portions at a fair price. Try the chicken and linguine or the grilled pork chops. Reservations accepted.

Open: 11 a.m.-9 p.m. M-F, 11 a.m-10 p.m. S, closed Su
Dress: casual ❖❖ MC V AmEx DI

FREMONT

Clay's Family Restaurant

7815 North 27 Lake George
Fremont, IN 46737
(219) 833-1332

*2 miles from I-80;
1 mile from I-69;
1 1/2 miles from
Horizon Outlet
Center.*

Daily all-you-can-eat fish, fried biscuits, fresh cobblers, and pies are especially tasty at Clay's, according to Angola officials who also praise the "warm, cozy atmosphere." Other popular specials include roast pork, roast turkey and roast beef. Sorry, no reservations.

Open: 11 a.m.-8 p.m. M-F, 7:30 a.m.-8 p.m. S-Su
Dress: casual   ❖❖

GARY

restaurant nominated by Gardest Gillespie, councilmember

The Beach Cafe

903 North Shelby Street
Gary, IN 46403
(219) 938-9890

Located in the lake-front area, the Beach Cafe serves first-rate steaks and seafood. The boned and buttered lake perch and the catfish served here are simply the best. Reservations advised.

Open: 11 a.m.-9:30p.m. M-Th, 11 a.m.-10:30 p.m. F-S,
2-8:30 p.m. Su
Dress: casual   ❖❖❖   **MC V AmEx Di DC**

Did you know?
The sole city in Indiana and the largest city in the nation founded in this century is Gary, created in 1906. It was named for Judge Elbert H. Gary, chairman of the board at U.S. Steel.

GOSHEN

restaurant nominated by Mike Puro, mayor

Olympia Candy Kitchen

136 North Main Street
Goshen, IN 46526
(219) 533-5040

Founded in 1912, the Olympia is a candy speciality shop and restaurant. The decor, including the wooden booths, reflects its proud heritage. This is a one-of-a-kind establishment located in downtown Goshen near city hall. Among the special treats is relishing the aroma of candy being made in the back room while enjoying dishes served at old-fashioned prices. The candy has been served to several U.S. Presidents, but you don't have to pay a king's ransom for it at the Olympia. Mayor Puro's favorite dish is the olive-nut sandwich. Don't leave Goshen without at least one box of the chocolate covered cashews. Sorry, no reservations.

**Open: 7 a.m.-5 p.m. M-T, Th-F, 7 a.m.-3:30 p.m. S,
7 a.m.-12:30 p.m. Su, closed W**
Dress: very casual ❖

GRIFFITH

restaurant nominated by Ronald Szafarczyk, councilmember;
Catherine Koschal, councilmember, Dyer

Stan's Steak & Seafood House

216 South Broad Street
Griffith, IN 46319
(219) 924-4767

Take I-94 to Cline, south on Cline to Ridge Rd., turn left and go 1 block to Broad St., then south on Broad St. 2 miles to Stan's.

"Try the steak," is the recommendation of Dyer Councilmember Koschal who enjoys the friendly atmosphere and accommodating staff at Stan's. For example, "the owner always seems to be around to assist you with whatever you need," she says. Councilmember Szafarczyk prefers the seafood platter and the perch, along with the steak. Reservations advised.

**Open: 11 a.m.-10 p.m. T-Th, 11 a.m.-11 p.m. F, 4-11 p.m. S,
noon-10 p.m. Su**
Dress: casual ❖❖❖ **MC V AmEx CB DC**

HAMMOND
restaurant nominated by Duane Dedelow, mayor

El Taco Real

935 Hoffman Street
Hammond, IN 46327
(219) 932-8333

20 min., from I-80/94; 5 min. from I-90.

For an authentic Mexican meal at a reasonable price, Mayor Dedelow suggests El Taco Real. It's off the beaten path in the oldest part of town, but well-worth the trip. His honor's favorite meal is the Fiesta plate. The pork tacos, burritos and other Mexican favorites are fabulous, too. Sorry, no reservations.
Open: 11 a.m.-11 p.m. Tu-Th, 11 a.m.-midnight F-S, closed S-M
Dress: casual   ❖❖   **MC V CB DI DC**

HEBRON
restaurant nominated by Emily Silich, councilmember, Hobart

Marti's Place at Ramsey's Landing

17519 North 700 West
Hebron, IN 46341
(219) 996-3363

Exit I-65 at SR 2, go east 7.5 miles to CR 625 S, then 1.5 miles to banks of Kankakee River.

With the appearance of an old country roadhouse, Marti's Place offers visitors a holiday atmosphere. Located on the Kankakee River, the restaurant is a favorite of Hobart Councilmember Silich because of its "fabulous" prime rib and seafood platter. Sorry, no reservations.
Open: 11 a.m.-10 p.m. Su-Th, 11 a.m.-11 p.m. F-S
Dress: casual   ❖❖

HOBART
restaurant nominated by Robert Malizzo, mayor

Country Lounge

3700 Montgomery
Hobart, IN 46342
(219) 942-6699

A local gathering spot for area business and political leaders, the Country Lounge is a favorite of several local officials, including Mayor Malizzo, who is partial to the Nikki salad and green bean soup. Portage Mayor Sammie Maletta recommends the lake

perch. Another favorite for the dietetically unrestricted is the
huge prime rib dinner. Reservations advised.
Open: 10 a.m.-midnight M-S, closed Su
Dress: dressy   ❖❖❖   **MC   V   AmEx   DC**

KNOX
restaurants nominated by Nancy Dembowski, mayor

Ernie's Fireside Inn

902 South Heaton
Knox, IN 46534
(219) 772-3746

Railroad fans will delight as the "G" gauge train whistles around
the dining room at Ernie's while guests enjoy some of the special
dishes available. Try the Onion Tree and one of their wide
variety of sandwiches. The pan-fried chicken livers are tempting,
too. Sorry, no reservations.
Open: 10 a.m.-11 p.m. M-S, closed Su
Dress: casual   ❖❖   **MC   V   AmEx   DI**

The Shore Club Restaurant

3698 South County Road 210
Knox, IN 46534
(219) 772-3363

Food prepared from scratch is the feature of the day, every day,
at the Shore Club. Mayor Dembowski says the beautiful view of
Bass Lake, the warm atmosphere and friendly employees make the
Sterling Silver Beef especially tasty. Reservations advised.
Open: 4-10 p.m. T-F, noon-10 p.m. S-Su, closed M
Dress: casual   ❖❖❖   **MC   V   AmEx   DI**

*The Shore Club is
located on Bass
Lake, the fourth-
largest natural lake
in Indiana.*

Did you know?
The main difference between a city and a town
is the separation of executive and legislative
functions. A town may become a city if its
population is more than 2,000.

KOUTS

restaurant nominated by Elaine Martin, clerk-treasurer

Birky's Cafe

205 South Main Street
Kouts, IN 46347
(219) 766-3851

Birky's is just 1/2 block south of the intersection of state roads 49 & 8.

Birky's Cafe is known for its fine Amish decor and delicious country food. Recommended selections include the broasted chicken, chicken and noodles and the barbecue ribs with homemade sauce. Clerk-Treasurer Martin says that the homemade pies are superb, and don't forget the giant cinnamon buns in the bakery. Reservations accepted.
Open: 7 a.m.-9 p.m. M-F, 6 a.m.-9 p.m. S-Su
Dress: casual ❖❖

LAKEVILLE

Jack's Bar & Grill

117 South Michigan Street
Lakeville, IN 46536
(219) 784-9939

A hometown bar and restaurant with a friendly small town-but-distinctly-Notre Dame atmosphere is why local officials say they prefer Jack's, located just seven miles south of the home of the "Fighting Irish." Recommendations include the deep fried shrimp and the chicken. Sorry, no reservations.
Open: 9 a.m.-11 p.m. M-S, closed Su
Dress: casual ❖❖

LOWELL

restaurants nominated by Marcia Carlson, clerk-treasurer

George's Family Restaurant

1910 East Commercial Avenue
Lowell, IN 46356
(219) 696-0313

A wide variety of Greek-American entrees is offered at George's, where Clerk-Treasurer Carlson says the homemade soups are among the best you'll find anywhere. Try George's omelette for breakfast. For lunch or dinner, the Italian beef or the chicken

shiskabob make excellent choices. Breakfast is served any time.
Reservations accepted.

Open: 6 a.m.-9 p.m. M-S, 6 a.m.-8 p.m. Su
Dress: casual ❖❖

The Hindquarter

1900 Lucas Parkway
Lowell, IN 46356
(219) 696-8344

There's nothing bland at The Hindquarter, where you can treat
yourself to some Cajun specialties. Popular items include the
New Orleans Cajun steak, sauteed walleye with basil tarragon
butter and the blackened rainbow trout. The barbecue ribs are a
winner, too, according to Clerk-Treasurer Carlson. Reservations
accepted.

Open: 4-10 p.m. T-Su, closed M
Dress: casual ❖❖ MC V

MERRILLVILLE

restaurant nominated by Jim Petalas, clerk-treasurer

The Odyssey Restaurant

7876 Broadway
Merrillville, IN 46140
(219) 738-2242

A friendly atmosphere and the best in Greek, American and
Italian cuisine at The Odyssey drew the attention and appetite of
Clerk-Treasurer Petalas. Try the broiled chicken fillet with rice
and vegetables or the chicken lemon rice soup. Also, don't miss
the homemade desserts from the bakery. Reservations accepted.

Open: 7 a.m.-11 p.m. daily
Dress: casual ❖ MC V

Did you know?
Merrillville is the state's most populated town,
with over 27,000 residents.

MICHIGAN CITY

restaurant nominated by Rose Marie Mannion, councilmember, Long Beach

The American Grill

5727 North 600 West
Michigan City, IN 46360
(219) 874-4603

You'll feel right at home at the American Grill, where you can choose from a variety of mouth watering items. Daily changes to the menu ensure there is always something new for you to try. You won't want to miss the rosemary roasted lamb loin with whipped sweet potatoes or the grilled salmon with creamy polenta and cilantro pesto. Reservations advised.
Open: 6-9 p.m. F-S
Dress: casual/dressy   ◆◆◆◆   **MC V AmEx DI**

restaurant nominated by Randall Miller, councilmember

Maxine & Heines Restaurant & Pub

521 Franklin Square
Michigan City, IN 46360
(219) 872-4500

Excellent steaks and succulent seafood have kept local folks satisfied with Maxine and Heines for over 40 years, declares Councilmember Miller. Try the top sirloin or the hickory grill. Reservations accepted.
Open: 11 a.m.-11 p.m. M-F, 4 p.m.-11 p.m. S, closed Su
Dress: casual   ◆◆◆   **MC V AmEx DC**

MIDDLEBURY

Das Dutchman Essenhaus
★ See Top Ten list, page 4 ★

★ See Top Ten list, page 4 ★

Did you know?
Indiana's first lighthouse still stands at Michigan City as a museum devoted to maritime artifacts.

MONTEREY

restaurant nominated by James Potthoff, clerk-treasurer

"World Famous" Corner Tavern

Main & Walnut
Monterey, IN 46960
(219) 542-9126

Just one block from the beautiful Tippecanoe River, the "World Famous" Corner Tavern is housed in a building erected in 1899. Local residents in the city frequent this restaurant for breakfast, business lunches, and dinner. Clerk-Treasurer Potthoff is especially fond of the sauteed perch. The sauteed walleye and fried chicken draw rave reviews, too. Reservations accepted.
Open: 7 a.m.-11 p.m. M-F, 7 a.m.-1 p.m. S, closed Su
Dress: casual ❖❖

Monterey is located 20 miles northwest of Rochester; 15 miles southeast of Knox; and 7 miles southwest of Culver.

MUNSTER

Giovanni's
★ See Top Ten list, page 3 ★

NAPPANEE

restaurant nominated by Ken Walters, mayor

Amish Acres Restaurant

1600 West Market, U.S. 6 West
Nappanee, IN 46550
(219) 773-4188 or 1-800-800-4942

A trip to north central Indiana is not complete without a visit to learn about the Indiana Amish heritage at Amish Acres. No visit to Amish Acres is complete without a fulfilling stop at its fine and expansive restaurant. Here Mayor Walters recommends the fried chicken and the bean soup. Ample parking is available immediately south of the restaurant. After eating, browse the gift shop for homemade breads and noodles, or, perhaps, an Amish quilt. Sorry, no reservations.
Open: 11 a.m.-7 p.m. M, 11 a.m.-7:30 p.m. T-S, 11 a.m.-6 p.m. Su from March 1-December 30
Dress: very casual ❖❖❖   **MC V Di DC**

Amish Acres is 1 mile west of SR 19 on U.S. 6 in Nappanee.

ORLAND
restaurant nominated by Marlene Walter, clerk-treasurer

Wall Lake Tavern

6100 North 1200 East Wall Lake
Orland, IN 46776
(219) 829-6335

Knotty pine and rustic accessories give the Wall Lake Tavern its old-fashioned charm. The stuffed walleye is Clerk-Treasurer Walter's favorite meal at the tavern, and the baked or fried walleye and fresh cut steaks are good choices. There are delicious homemade soups, a fresh salad bar and gourmet coffees available, too. Reservations accepted.
Open: 10 a.m.-11 p.m. M-S, closed Su
Dress: casual   ❖❖

OSCEOLA
restaurant nominated by Jerry DeDapper, councilmember, Mishawaka

Between-The-Buns

1720 Lincoln Way West
Osceola, IN 46561
(219) 679-4474

If you're a sports fan, be sure to stop at Between-The-Buns, which specializes in unique sandwiches and is home to "the best hot wings in the area." One of Mishawaka Councilmember DeDapper's favorites is the "Ryne Sandburger." The menu features a Hamburger Hall of Fame, the Wide World of Sandwedges and a list of salads from the Greens Keeper. Try the Holy Cow Burger, Pistol Pete's Bayou Bird (Cajun spiced deep fried chicken) or the Good Year Shrimp. Reservations accepted.
Open: 11 a.m.-10 p.m. M-F, noon-midnight S-Su
Dress: very casual   ❖   **MC V AmEx DI**

Did you know?
The first African-American mayor of a medium-sized city was Richard D. Hatcher, elected to the top office in Gary, a city of about 90,000, in November 1967.

PLYMOUTH

restaurants nominated by Jack Greenlee, mayor

The Brass Rail Restaurant & Lounge

225 North Michigan Street
Plymouth, IN 46563
(219) 936-7004

Take Plymouth Exit from U.S. 30 or U.S. 31 and head downtown.

A casual atmosphere welcomes visitors to the Brass Rail in the heart of downtown Plymouth, where steaks and seafood are the house specialties. Mayor Greenlee recommends the buttered lake perch. You may want to try the Cajun orange roughy, sauteed lake perch, fresh seafood alfredo or their always famous hand-breaded cod. Reservations accepted.

Open: 11 a.m.-10 p.m. M-F, 11 a.m.-10:30 p.m. S, closed Su
Dress: casual ❖❖ MC V DI

Christo's Family Dining

2227 North Michigan Avenue
Plymouth, IN 46563
(219) 935-5100

Regardless of the season it's always spring at Christo's where fresh flowers are displayed daily. Mayor Greenlee satisfies his appetite with roast pork and dressing, topped off with a piece of delicious homemade pie or cake. Reservations accepted.

Open: 6 a.m.-midnight daily
Dress: very casual ❖❖ MC V

PORTAGE

restaurant nominated by Sammie Maletta, mayor

The Savoy Supper Club

2542 Portage Mall
Portage, IN 46368
(219) 762-4114

A favorite dining place of Mayor Maletta, the Savoy features steaks and Italian-American dishes. According to his honor, "the manicotti is outstanding." Nightly entertainment enhances the pleasure of dining guests. Reservations advised.

Open: 4-10 p.m. Tu, Th; 4-12:30 a.m. W; 4-11:30 p.m. F-S
(cocktail lounge open until 2 a.m. F-S); closed M
Dress: casual ❖❖ MC V AmEx DC

RENSSELAER

City Office & Pub

114 South Van Rensselaer
Rensselaer, IN 47978

The City Office & Pub is just west of the courthouse.

This is *the* local haunt of politicians and business leaders, with political memorabilia, a deer's head and an old juke box among the eclectic assortment of adornments. Special recommendations here include the Friday seafood chowder special, prime rib, and shrimp stir fry. Reservations advised.
Open: 11 a.m.-10 p.m. M-Th, 11 a.m.-11 p.m. F-S, closed Su
Dress: casual/dressy   ❖❖

ROCHESTER

restaurant nominated by Edward Fansler, mayor

Evergreen Cafe

530 Main Street
Rochester, IN 46975
(219) 223-1809

Every Indiana town has a place where farmers, business leaders and retirees convene to swap gossip and ponder the issues of the day. In Rochester, according to Mayor Fansler, that place is the Evergreen Cafe. Between the consulting sessions, Mayor Fansler recommends the breaded tenderloin. Sorry, no reservations.
Open: 5:30 a.m.-2 p.m. M-F, 5:30-10 a.m. S, closed Su
Dress: very casual   ❖

ST. JOHN

restaurants nominated by Kenneth Gembala, councilmember

Apollo Family Restaurant

9141 Wicker Avenue
St. John, IN 46373
(219) 365-8733

Apollo is 3 miles from SR 30 in the St. John Mall.

Breakfast, lunch and dinner specials galore grace the menu at Apollo Family Restaurant, where you'll find American, Italian and Greek selections. Councilmember Gembala suggests the steaks and salads. Reservations advised.
Open: 6 a.m.-10 p.m. daily, closed Christmas and Thanksgiving
Dress: casual/dressy   ❖❖   MC V AmEx

Dick's Restaurant

10808 Wicker Avenue
St. John, IN 46373
(219) 365-5041

Although they claim the "best jumbo shrimp and lake perch around," Dick's offers visitors a dinner menu loaded with other mouth watering selections. The lunch specials aren't bad, either. Reservations advised, especially on weekends.
Open: 4-10 p.m. M-T, 11:30 a.m.-10 p.m. W-Th,
11:30 a.m.-11 p.m. F-S, noon-9 p.m. Su
Dress: casual   ❖❖❖   **MC V DI**

SCHERERVILLE

restaurant nominated by Ronald Szafarczyk, councilmember, Griffith;
Catherine Koschal, councilmember, Dyer

Teibel's

1775 Route 41
Schererville, IN 46375
(219) 865-2000

Teibel's is located at the intersection of U.S. 30 and U.S. 41.

Buttered lake perch, fried chicken and frog legs have made Teibel's famous, say area councilmembers Szafarczyk and Koschal. A large restaurant with capacity for up to 500 patrons, Teibel's has been a regional favorite for decades. Reservations advised.
Open: 11 a.m.-10 p.m. Su-Th, 11 a.m.-11 p.m. F-S
Dress: casual/dressy   ❖❖❖   **MC V AmEx CB DC**

SOUTH BEND

East Bank Emporium Restaurant

121 South Niles Avenue
South Bend, IN 46617
(219) 234-9000

Ask for a table with a view of the scenic St. Joseph River at the Emporium before enjoying the local favorite: the chicken pita pocket and a salad. The prime rib dinner is a winner, too. Reservations accepted.
Open: 11 a.m.-9 p.m. M-F, 11 a.m.-10 p.m. S, 4-9 p.m. Su
Dress: casual   ❖❖❖ **MC V AmEx CB DI DC**

TOPEKA

restaurants nominated by A.F. Haggard, councilmember
Tom Miller, councilmember

The Country Inn

110 Redman Drive
Topeka, IN 46571
(219) 593-2515

Enjoy Amish-prepared food, especially the stuffed chicken breast and hand-dipped cod, at the Country Inn. Be sure to save room for a piece of homemade pie. The Sunday morning breakfasts are excellent. Reservations accepted.

Open: 5 a.m.-2 p.m. M-S, 7 a.m.-2 p.m. Su
Dress: very casual ❖

Tiffany's

P.O. Box 247
East Lake Street
Topeka, IN 46571
(219) 593-2988

Tiffany's is three blocks east of the stop light on Lake St.

While it's not a jewelry store, you can expect some real gems on the menu at Tiffany's. They specialize in old-fashioned good cooking, according to Councilmember Haggard, who recommends the Swiss steak and homemade pies. Wednesdays feature an all-you-can-eat fish dinner. Reservations accepted.

Open: 6 a.m.-7 p.m. M, 6 a.m.-8 p.m. T-S, closed Su
Dress: very casual ❖

VALPARAISO

restaurants nominated by David Butterfield, mayor

Restaurante Don Quijote

119 Lincolnway
Valparaiso, IN 46383
(219) 462-7976

One of the very best (and only) Spanish restaurants in Indiana, according to Mayor Butterfield, is the Don Quijote, which daily draws patrons from four states. In addition to the exciting Spanish cuisine, weekend diners are often treated to Flamenco dancing. Mayor Butterfield's favorite meal is the "Pinchos Morunos," Moorish style skewered veal and pork marinated in wine and spices. Reservations advised, especially on weekends.

Open: 11:30 a.m.-2:30 p.m. M-F, 5-9:30 p.m. M-Th,
5-11 p.m. F-S, closed Su
Dress: casual/dressy   ❖❖❖ MC V AmEx CB DI DC

The Strongbow Inn

2405 U.S. Highway 30 East
Valparaiso, IN 46383
(219) 462-5121

Named for Potawatomi Indian Chief Strongbow, the Strongbow
Inn offers the finest in continental cuisine. You'll gobble up the
large variety of turkey dishes offered here. Councilmember Dale
Bucker from nearby Wanatah especially enjoys Strongbow's
Turkey Pie. Reservations advised.

The Strongbow Inn is near Carlton Lodge at the intersection of U.S. 30 and SR 49.

Open: 11 a.m.-9 p.m. M-F, 11 a.m.-9:30 p.m. S,
11 a.m.-8:30 p.m. Su
Dress: casual/dressy   ❖❖❖ MC V AmEx CB DI DC

WAKARUSA

Come and Dine

66402 State Road 19
Wakarusa, IN 46573
(219) 862-2714

People of all ages will enjoy the wide variety of Amish dishes
and the full-size train that carries passengers to a museum at Come
and Dine. Try the roast beef, and don't miss the homemade
cakes and cookies.

Open: 6 a.m.-9 p.m. M-S, closed Su
Dress: casual   ❖❖

restaurant nominated by Laurelyn Street, councilmember

Cook's Pizza

101 South Elkhart
Wakarusa, IN 46573
(219) 802-4425

A typical "small town restaurant" with pizza that is "out of this
world," is the way Councilmember Street describes Cook's. Try
the stromboli sandwiches, too. Reservations accepted.

Open: 11 a.m.-9 p.m. M-F, 11 a.m.-11 p.m. S, 4-10 p.m. Su
Dress: very casual   ❖

ViewPoint Restaurant

935 North Detroit Street
Warsaw, IN 46580
(219) 269-1001

ViewPoint is located one mile south of U.S. 30 on SR 15.

Full glass frontage and mirrored walls give patrons of ViewPoint Restaurant a panoramic view of beautiful Center Lake. The house specialty is prime rib, and one of the local favorites is the lobster and pasta. There also is a scrumptious Sunday brunch. Reservations advised.

Open: 10 a.m.-2 p.m. , 5-10 p.m. M-S; 10 a.m.-2 p.m. Su
Dress: casual   ❖❖❖   **MC V AmEx**

Wolfgang's Restaurant

617 South Buffalo Street
Warsaw, IN 46580
(219) 269-6678

The fresh seafood and the veal dishes have made Wolfgang's a popular choice for local and out-of-town diners. Located at the south end of Warsaw, the restaurant boasts an amicable staff which makes the meals even more enjoyable. Reservations advised.

Open: 11 a.m.-2 p.m., 5-10 p.m. T-F, 5-10 p.m. S, closed Su-M
Dress: casual   ❖❖❖/❖❖❖❖   **MC V**

Western Indiana's covered bridges are gateways to history

Take a trip back in time to Western Indiana, where ancient covered bridges serve as gateways, transporting travelers by quaint maple sugar farms, restored grist mills and through centuries in time to Indiana's early history.

The 32 authentic covered bridges of Parke County, dating from 1856 to 1920, are a delight to explore...for each has a story to tell. If you prefer a self-guided tour, pick up a map at the Tourist Information Center located on Hwy. 36 in Rockville's 1883-built Railroad Depot.

But, don't overlook what's between the bridges. To the east of county seat Rockville is Billie Creek Village, a recreated 1900s community, featuring craft demonstrations, 30 historic buildings and wagon rides.

Antiquing has been the recent rage in the Brazil and Terre Haute areas with numerous shops offering the possibility of finding bargains on ancient treasures.

One of Terre Haute's many delightful diversions is a walking tour of Farrington's Grove, among the city's first neighborhoods, where you can see a genuine Lustron House, built entirely of metal.

Just north of Terre Haute is St. Mary-of-The-Woods College where a restful tour of the attractive campus should include Our Lady of Lourdes Grotto, a replica of the famous shrine in France.

At Dana, near the Illinois border, Pulitzer Prize winning World War II correspondent Ernie Pyle is remembered in a recently-expanded museum and shrine to the beloved Hoosier newsman. Call (317) 665-3633 for details about the museum.

Monticello offers a small-town resort atmosphere with big entertainment thrills at Indiana Beach Amusement Park where the Hoosier Hurricane Roller Coaster, camping, lodging, and a water park should stimulate your appetite.

The Lafayette/West Lafayette

area offers a variety of exciting alternatives, including a nostalgic visit to Lafayette's Columbian Park with 1950s era rides, paddleboats and petting zoo.

Battle Ground, north of Lafayette, provides access to one of the most dramatic clashes between Native Americans and U.S. troops. The Battle Ground Interpretive Center and scenic parklike surroundings contrast with the bloody conflict which raged here in 1811 when Gen. William Henry Harrison's troops were attacked by a band of Shawnees led by The Prophet from nearby Prophetstown.

Swing over to Attica, once a port on the Wabash and Erie Canal, where several century-old downtown buildings have been restored, including the Attica Hotel Antique Mall.

The nation's only publicly displayed German V-1 Buzz Bomb rests on the Greencastle Courthouse Square, which also boasts a bank once robbed by 1920s desperado John Dillinger, and one of the first drug stores owned by pharmaceutical giant, Eli Lilly.

These are but a few appetizers for what lies beyond the covered bridges of western Indiana. For more information, contact the following visitor information centers:

Attica	(317) 762-2511
Brazil	(812) 448-8457
Clinton	(317) 832-3844
Frankfort	(317) 654-5507
Greater Lafayette	(317) 447-9999
Logansport	(219) 362-5200
Montgomery County	(317) 362-5200
Monticello	(219) 583-7220
Parke County	(317) 569-5226
Putnam County	(317) 653-8743
Spencer	(812) 829-3245
Sullivan County	(812) 268-4836
Terre Haute	(812) 234-5555

BATTLE GROUND

restaurant nominated by Geraldine Berghoff, clerk-treasurer

TC's Restaurant & Tavern

109 North Railroad
Battle Ground, IN 47290
(317) 567-2838

Relax in the atmosphere of the 1960s at TC's Restaurant &
Tavern. It's the social gathering and dining place for area
residents, Clerk-Treasurer Berghoff says. She recommends you try
the boneless country-style barbecue ribs. Reservations accepted.

*TC's is a block
north of Main St.
by the railroad
tracks.*

Open: 11 a.m.-10 p.m. M-F, 11 a.m.-midnight S, closed Su
Dress: very casual ❖❖

BRAZIL

restaurants nominated by Ken Crabb, mayor; Jim Sheese, councilmember

Blue Bonnet

903 West Jackson Street
Brazil, IN 47834
(812) 442-1233

A local institution drawing patrons from far and wide, including
Mayor Crabb and Councilmember Sheese, the Blue Bonnet's
patriotic and historic decorations create a warm and healthy
nonsmoking atmosphere in which to enjoy the specialties of the
house, like their delicious barbecue ribs. Reservations accepted.

Open: 7 a.m.-8 p.m. M-S, 11 a.m.-2 p.m. Su
Dress: casual ❖/❖❖ **MC V**

Company's Coming

303 North Forest Avenue
Brazil, IN 47834
(812) 443-7963

You'll feel right at home when you enter Company's Coming and
are greeted by the beautiful handcrafted woodwork which graces
the interior. It's the perfect setting to try the supreme salad and
chicken pot pie. Mayor Crabb recommends you save room for a
slice of banana split pie. Reservations advised.

*Look for the large
Victorian home two
blocks north of U.S.
40 on SR 59.*

Open: 11 a.m.-2 p.m. T-F, 6-8 p.m. S (by reservation only)
also open special holiday hours throughout the year
Dress: casual/dressy ❖❖/❖❖❖

CAYUGA

The Covered Bridge Restaurant

Route 1
Cayuga, IN 47928

Located in a historic merchant's building adjacent to a covered bridge, the Covered Bridge Restaurant is a favorite of many local and out-of-town visitors. Look over the display of license plates from all 50 states and many Canadian provinces while you enjoy the catfish dinner, a house specialty. And be sure to try a piece of one of their 12 homemade pies. Sorry, no reservations.
Open: 11 a.m.-9 p.m. M-F, 8 a.m.-9 p.m. S-Su
Dress: casual   ◆◆

Logan 105

105 Logan Street
Cayuga, IN 47928
(317) 492-4477

Head west on 234 to the Logan 105 sign, go south about 3 blocks to a blue building with blue awnings.

Logan 105 has "the best taco salad around," according to local officials. Located in an old converted warehouse, the restaurant features pan fried chicken on Sundays and fish on Fridays. Reservations accepted for groups of 10 or more.
Open: 5 a.m.-7 p.m. M-F, 7 a.m.-2 p.m. S-Su
Dress: very casual   ◆◆

CENTENARY

restaurant nominated by Phyllis Lambert, clerk-treasurer, Fairview Park

Natale's Cuisine

Route 3, Box 714 A
Clinton, IN 47842
(317) 832-6068

From SR 63 go west on Hwy. 163 about 2.5 miles.

Located near the Illinois border, west of Clinton, Natale's Cuisine specializes in Italian dishes. Clerk-Treasurer Lambert recommends you try the spaghetti. And don't hesitate to bend the ears of owners Jim and Bobbie Natale when they stop at your table.   Reservations accepted.
Open: 4:30-9 p.m. T-F, 11a.m.-9 p.m. S, closed Su-M
Dress: very casual   ◆◆

> *Did you know?*
> 64% of Hoosiers live in cities and towns.

Junction One Stop Restaurant

Rural Route 2
Center Point, IN 47841
(812) 835-3112 or 835-2644

Daily plate lunches are the specialty of the house at Junction One Stop Restaurant. Fridays feature all-you-can-eat fish, and all weekend long you can get mouth-watering ribeye steak dinners for $7.99. Former Celtics star and native Hoosier Larry Bird has been known to dine at the Junction, but they say they like to serve the locals and tourists alike. Reservations accepted for groups or parties.

Open: 24-hours daily
Dress: casual   ❖/❖❖   **MC V AmEx DI**

5 miles south of Brazil Exit on I-70 at the junction of state roads 59 and 46.

WESTERN

CLAY CITY

Main Street Diner

721 Main Street
Clay City, IN 47841
(812) 939-3245

As its name suggests, the Main Street Diner offers home-style meals and is especially proud of its sumptuous buffet offered from 10:30 a.m. to 1 p.m. on Fridays, Saturdays and Sundays. Local officials recommend the broasted chicken. Sorry, no reservations.

Open: 5 a.m.-1:30 p.m. M-F, 6 a.m.-1:30 p.m. S-Su
Dress: very casual   ❖

The Firehouse Restaurant

711 Main Street
Clay City, IN 47841
(812) 939-3205

You won't find anything alarming about the Firehouse Restaurant. What you will find is some outstanding cooking; everything from pizza and breaded tenderloin sandwiches to seafood and Italian specials. There is a daily lunch buffet, and breakfast is served daily until 11 a.m., too. Reservations accepted.

Open: 5:30 a.m.-10 p.m. daily
Dress: very casual   ❖

15 minutes from I-70 on SR 59 in Clay City's business district.

CLINTON

restaurant nominated by Phyllis Lambert, clerk-treasurer, Fairview Park

Zamberlettis at the Castle

1600 North Seventh Street
Clinton, IN 47842
(317) 832-8811

Exquisite Italian cuisine is the hallmark of the Castle, according to Fairview Park Clerk-Treasurer Lambert. Her favorites are the garlic shrimp and chicken dinner, but anything made by the northern Italian family who owns this establishment is tempting. Reservations accepted.

Open: 11 a.m.-2 p.m. T-S, 5-9 p.m. W-F, 4-9 p.m. S
11 a.m.-7 p.m. Su, closed M
Dress: casual   ◆◆   **MC V DI**

COLFAX

Miller's Fish Suppers
★ See Top Ten list, page 3 ★

COVINGTON

restaurants nominated by Henry Schmitt, councilmember;
J.H. Robinson, councilmember, Newtown

The Beef House
★ See Top Ten list, page 1 ★

Maple Corner

1126 Liberty Street
Covington, IN 47932
(317) 793-2224

A unique dining experience awaits visitors and antique lovers at Maple Corner, where Councilmember Schmitt recommends the fresh baked breads, salads and the barbecued pork chops. Maple Corner also is the out-of-town favorite of Newtown Councilmember Robinson, who recommends the fish and steaks. Reservations advised.

Open: 4:30-9 p.m. M-Th, 4:30-10 p.m. F-S,
11:30 a.m.-8:30 p.m. Su
Dress: casual   ◆◆◆   **MC V AmEx DI**

DANA

restaurant nominated by Irene J. Wesley, clerk-treasurer

R&R Junction

State Road 36 & 71
Dana, IN 47847

When you're through visiting the Ernie Pyle museum, take time to dine in a former railroad dining car. The home-cooked food comes fast and is delivered by friendly servers at the R&R Junction, where Clerk-Treasurer Wesley highly recommends the fish and spaghetti dishes. Reservations accepted.

Open: 6 a.m.-2 p.m. M-S, closed Su
Dress: casual ❖

GREENCASTLE

restaurant nominated by Susan Murray, councilmember

Almost Home Tea Room

17 West Franklin
Greencastle, IN 46135
(317) 653-5788

Located in Greencastle's historic downtown square, the Almost Home Tea Room has beautiful country crafts, teas and antique amenities. The homemade soups, daily entrees and desserts are outstanding. Reservations accepted.

Open: 10 a.m.-6 p.m. M-F, 10 a.m.-5 p.m. S
Dress: casual ❖ MC V DI

A Different Drummer

★ See Top Ten list, page 4 ★

restaurant nominated by Mike Harmless, mayor

Hathaway's

18 South Jackson Street
Greencastle, IN 46135
(317) 635-1228

1/2 block south of the courthouse square on Jackson St.

History abounds at Hathaway's, where dishes are named after local places and events. Try the Jackson Street chicken, or any one of their delicious menu items. Reservations accepted (except Fridays and Saturdays).

Open: 11 a.m.-9 p.m. M-Th, 11 a.m.-11 p.m. F-S, noon-8 p.m. Su
Dress: casual ❖❖ MC V AmEx DI

restaurant nominated by Michael Rokicki, councilmember

Jackson Family Restaurant
Double Decker Drive-In

11058 Indianapolis Road
Greencastle, IN 46135
(317) 653-4302

*Located on
Indianapolis Rd.
across from First
Citizens Bank.*

Stop by the Double Decker Drive-In, where the chicken and
reuben are special favorites of Councilmember Rokicki. The
broasted chicken double decker is popular, too. Reservations
accepted.
Open: 7 a.m.-9 p.m. daily
Dress: casual ❖❖ **MC V AmEx Di**

MONTICELLO

restaurant nominated by Richard Cronch, mayor

Beaver Dam Inn

1200 Francis Street
Monticello, IN 49760
(219) 583-8375

*from SR 39 North,
go to CR 175 and
head west to Norway
Dam; go south 2
blocks to Beaver
Dam.*

Anyone who walks through the doors is considered family at the
Beaver Dam Inn, where excellent seafood and steaks are the
specialty of the house; or try one of the nightly specials. Enjoy
the beautiful antique wall hangings, and take a look at the ceiling
made of egg crates. Reservations advised.
Open: 4-10 p.m. W-S (January-April),
4-11 p.m. T-S (May-December), closed Su-M
Dress: casual ❖❖❖ **MC V**

NEW ROSS

restaurant nominated by Rebecca L. Lowe, clerk-treasurer

New Ross Steak House

Main Street
New Ross, IN 46968
(317) 723-9291

Enjoy hand-cut steaks and delicious sandwiches at New Ross
Steak House. Clerk-Treasurer Lowe says they serve some of the
best steaks in Indiana at some of the most reasonable prices. She
suggests the sirloin. Reservations accepted.
Open: 9 a.m.-9 p.m. T-F, 9 a.m.-10 p.m. S, closed Su-M
Dress: very casual ❖❖❖

WESTERN

ROSEDALE

restaurant nominated by Vicki Oldham, clerk-treasurer

Harvest House

202 North Main Street
Rosedale, IN 47874
(317) 548-1102

Take U.S. 41 North to Parke/Vigo County Line Rd., and go east to Rosedale.

Located in the heart of covered bridge country, the Harvest House offers diners a choice of exquisite sandwiches and great daily specials according to Clerk-Treasurer Oldham. She suggests the fried chicken, chicken and noodles and the meatloaf. Don't forget to try the homemade desserts. Reservations accepted.
Open: 6 a.m.-2 p.m. M-S plus 5-9 p.m. F, 11 a.m.-3 p.m. Su
Dress: casual   ❖

WEST LAFAYETTE

restaurant nominated by Sonya Margerum, mayor

Heisei

1048 Sagamore Parkway West
West Lafayette, IN 47906
(317) 465-1682

Diners are greeted by Kimono-clad waitresses at this authentic Japanese restaurant, where Mayor Margerum marvels at the beautiful wood-highlight decor. The mayor's recommendation: sushi. Reservations advised.
Open: 11:30 a.m.-1:30 p.m. T-F, 5-10 p.m. T-Th, 5-11 p.m. S,
5-9 p.m. Su, closed M
Dress: casual/dressy   ❖   **MC   V   AmEx   Di   DC**

Did you know?
Elected officials at the local level provide many of our most critical services such as utilities, roads, police and fire protection.

Sarge Oaks

721 Main Street
West Lafayette, IN 47906
(317) 742-5230

On Main Street, a main attraction to many locals is Sarge Oaks.
Mayor Margerum suggests you consider the variety of steaks and
spaghetti dishes offered, and don't leave without sampling the
"wonderful" raspberry pie. Reservations accepted (advised on
weekends).
Open: 11 a.m.-2p.m., 4:30-9:30 p.m. T-Th;
11 a.m.-2 p.m., 4:30-9:45 p.m. F, 4:30-9:45 p.m. S, closed Su-M
Dress: casual   ❖❖❖   MC   V   AmEx   DI

Did you know?
The covered bridge on the Rockville golf
course makes it the only fairway in the known
golf world to have a covered bridge over a
waterway.

Eastern Indiana attractions beckon from a bygone age

Eastern Indiana's abundance of intriguing restaurants are complemented by a wealth of entertainment centers, museums, heritage, tourism, shopping, and scenic diversions.

The area is home to Garfield the Cat, Johnny Appleseed and the father of flight, Wilbur Wright. This former home of four major Native American tribes also boasts the nation's newest Abraham Lincoln Museum in Fort Wayne (opening Oct. 1995). At Huntington, a museum honors a latter-day White House resident, former Vice President Dan Quayle, and the late actor James Dean is remembered at a museum in Fairmount. But Indiana's true heroes are preserved for eternal reverence in New Castle at the Indiana Basketball Hall of Fame where such Hoosier roundball luminaries as Larry Bird, Oscar Robertson, Rick Mount, and John Wooden are enshrined.

Many of the nation's automobiles were produced in this area prior to World War I, and , if you're nostalgic, you'll delight in the classic glamour of 140 vintage, antique and special interest motor vehicles at the Auburn-Cord-Duesenberg Museum located in the original Auburn Motor Car Company building in Auburn.

Plan to spend some extra time, too, at area entertainment centers such as Bearcreek Farms, a 200-acre farm which offers family dining, lodging and

a theater. Amishville, located four miles south of Berne, is situated on a 120-acre operating farm and offers tours and buggy rides to present the Amish way of life. Stop at the 21-acre Swiss Heritage Village in Berne, where the world's largest cider press is on display.

Shopping adventures range from the antique shops of Centerville to the new outlet mall at Daleville.

These are but a few of the hundreds of exciting opportunities awaiting visitors to Eastern Indiana. For details and additional information, contact the local visitor bureaus listed on the following page:

35

Anderson	(317) 643-5633 or 1-800-53-ENJOY
Auburn	(219) 925-2100
Berne	(219) 589-8080
Bluffton	(219) 824-0510
Connersville	(317) 825-2561
Decatur	(219) 724-2604
Fort Wayne	(219) 424-3700 or 1-800-767-7752
Hartford City	(317) 348-1905
Huntington	(219) 359-TOUR or 1-800-848-4282
Kendallville	(219) 347-1554
Kokomo	(317) 457-6802 or 1-800-837-0971
Marion	(317) 668-5435 or 1-800-662-9474
Muncie	(317) 284-2700 or 1-800-568-6862
New Castle	(317) 521-4302 or 1-800-676-4302
Peru	(317) 472-1923
Portland	(219) 726-4481
Richmond	(317) 935-8687 or 1-800-828-8414
Rushville	(317) 932-2880
Tipton	(317) 675-7533
Wabash	(219) 563-1168
Winchester	(317) 584-3266

ALBANY

restaurant nominated by William Conn, clerk-treasurer

Osborn's St. Clair Restaurant

220 West State Street
Albany, IN 47320
(317) 789-8487

Clerk-Treasurer Conn declares Osborn's is "a great place for a
relaxing family outing," because of the great home-cooked meals,
reasonable prices and attentive servers. Try the ribs or beef and
noodles. Conn says he can't resist the homemade pies, and you
won't be able to, either. Sorry, no reservations.

Open: 5 a.m.-7 p.m. M-F, 5:30 a.m.-1:30 p.m. S, closed Su
Dress: casual   ❖

ALEXANDRIA

restaurants nominated by Ed Schmidt, mayor

EASTERN

Hi-way Cafe

State Road 9 North
Alexandria, IN 46001
(317) 724-9969

Hi-way Cafe is 2 miles south of Alexandria on SR 9.

"Drop by anytime," is the invitation from Mayor Schmidt. That's
because the Hi-way Cafe is open 24 hours a day, 365 days a
year. Thanks to the great food and reasonable prices, Schmidt
says local folks drop in frequently and linger after a hearty meal to
savor the delicious peanut butter pie. Reservations accepted.
Open: 24 hours, daily
Dress: very casual   ❖

Alexandria Bakery

110 North Harrison
Alexandria, IN 46001
(317) 724-7367

Although they are known for such tempting delicacies as their
carmel rolls, the Bakery's luncheon specials are irresistible, too,
Mayor Schmidt says. He recommends the ham and beans, but
says the chicken and noodles are mouth watering also. Sorry, no
reservations.

Open: 5:30 a.m.-5:30 p.m. M-F, 5:30 a.m.-4 p.m. S, closed Su
Dress: casual   ❖

ANDERSON

restaurants nominated by J. Mark Lawler, mayor

Lucy's

2460 East County Road 67
Anderson, IN 46017
(317) 643-3144

This is the place for a hearty breakfast, and where the mayor visits every morning to hear the latest gossip while accepting advice on how to run the city from the "regulars" at Lucy's. His favorite is a special breakfast platter of eggs, sausage, bacon, potatoes, and toast. The country pot roast and homemade chicken and noodle dinners are appetizing as well. Reservations accepted.
Open: 6:30 a.m.-8:30 p.m. daily
Dress: casual   ❖

Homestretch Restaurant at Hoosier Park

4500 Dan Patch Boulevard
Anderson, IN 46013
(317) 683-2585

From I-69 take Exit 26 and go north to 53rd St., turn right and go 2 blocks to Hoosier Park.

For an exciting dining experience, Mayor Lawler suggests the Homestretch Restaurant located at Hoosier Park, Indiana's first pari-mutuel horse racing track. Diners can view the best in live and simulcast horse racing from televisions at each table. The mayor's hot tip for a good meal is the stuffed pork chops. The Sunday brunch buffet also is a winner. Reservations advised.
Open: 11 a.m.-5 p.m. M, 11 a.m.-5 p.m. W-S,
11 a.m.-5:30 p.m. Su, Closed T
Dress: casual   ❖❖❖   **MC V AmEx DI DC**

AUBURN

restaurants nominated by Norman N. Rohm, mayor

Joshua's Restaurant & Lounge

640 North Grandstaff Drive
Auburn, IN 46706
(219) 925-4407

Take Exit 129 off I-69 and head east to the second stoplight, then turn left.

From the minute you step into the plant-filled atrium at Joshua's Restaurant and Lounge, you know that you'll be treated like a special guest. Excellent daily specials fill the menu, or you may want to try a mouth-watering steak or the authentic German style food. Joshua's is an excellent place for business luncheons and dinners. Reservations advised on the weekends.

Open: 11 a.m.-10 p.m. M-F, 4 p.m.-11 p.m. S, closed Su
Dress: casual   ❖❖/❖❖❖   **MC   V   AmEx   DI**

AVILLA

restaurant nominated by John DeLuceney, councilmember; and Jean Traxler, clerk-treasurer

St. James Restaurant & Lounge

204 East Albion Street
Avilla, IN 46710
(219) 897-2114

St. James is 9 miles west of the Auburn Exit on I-69.

Located in a renovated historic hotel, the St. James Restaurant & Lounge is operated by the William Freeman family, who converted the facility to a restaurant in 1949. Clerk-Treasurer Traxler and Councilmember DeLuceney are especially fond of the broasted chicken, codfish, and barbecue ribs. Reservations accepted during the week.

Open: 7 a.m.-11 p.m. M-Th, 7 a.m.-midnight F-S, closed Su
Dress: casual   ❖❖   **MC   V**

BLUFFTON

restaurant nominated by Mary E. Smith, councilmember, Poneto

The Dutch Mill

402 North Main
Bluffton, IN 46714
(317) 824-4000

For nearly a half-century, the Dutch Mill has been serving up home-cooked meals in a relaxing environment. Nearby Poneta Town Councilmember Mary Smith recommends the breaded tenderloin sandwich. Other popular items include baked steak, pork brains and fried rabbit. Reservations accepted.

Open: 11 a.m.-10 p.m. M-F, closed S-Su and holidays
Dress: very casual   ❖❖

Did you know?
Mayors and town clerk-treasurers have the power to solemnize marriages.

CENTERVILLE

Jag's Cafe

129 East Main Street
Centerville, IN 47330
(317) 855-2282

Take Exit 146 off I-70 and head south 4 miles, turn left at the traffic light and go about 1/2 block.

Located in historic Centerville, Jag's Cafe offers delightful dining in a unique atmosphere featuring antiques, including the bar and back bar from the 1895 Chicago World's Fair, and numerous autographed guitars and photos of contemporary stars. Local officials recommend you try one of the house specialties: French onion soup. Don't miss the cheesecake—guaranteed to satisfy your sweet tooth! Reservations advised.

Open: 11 a.m.-9 p.m. Su-Th, 11 a.m.-11 p.m. F-S
Dress: casual ◆◆◆ **MC V DI**

The Station Stop

Webb's Antique Mall
200 Union Street
Centerville, IN 47330
(317) 855-2489

Take a break from antique hunting at the Station Stop restaurant, located in the world's largest antique mall. The Station Stop serves appetizing homemade soups and gourmet sandwiches. You won't want to miss the great homemade pies. Sorry, no reservations.

Open: 10 a.m.-4 p.m. daily, closed Thanksgiving and Christmas
Dress: very casual ◆

CONNERSVILLE

restaurants nominated by Marion Newhouse, mayor

Conner House Smorgasbord

3542 Western Avenue
Connersville, IN 47331
(317) 827-0059

This is an exciting place to dine after a 30-mile Whitewater Valley scenic steam locomotive trip between Connersville and Metamora, declares Mayor Newhouse. Located in a former bowling alley, the observant diner will note that the tables have been made from old bowling lane strips. The mayor recommends

the fried chicken and any of the wide assortment of tasty desserts. You won't strike out with Friday's seafood buffet, either. Reservations accepted for parties of 10 or more.
**Open: 4:30 -8 p.m. Th, 4:30-8:30 p.m. F, 4-9 p.m. S,
11 a.m.-6:30 p.m. Su**
Dress: casual   ◆◆◆   **MC V**

Miller's Cafeteria

704 North Eastern Avenue
Connersville, IN 47331
(317) 825-6821

Mayor Newhouse advises that Miller's is one of the most popular eating places in Connersville. It's where the local civic clubs hold their luncheon meetings—always a sure sign of a quality restaurant. The mayor's favorite dishes here are the ham and the vinegar slaw. Reservations accepted.
Open: 11 a.m.-8:30 p.m. Su-Th, 11 a.m.-9 p.m. F-S
Dress: very casual   ◆

Willow's Restaurant

522 Central Avenue
Connersville, IN 47331
(317) 825-5552

Follow SR 1 from north or south to 6th and Eastern; go west 1 block; and turn left.

"Warm and cozy" with a wide assortment of delights displayed at the lunch deli buffet are positive features of Willow's, according to Mayor Newhouse. The buffet is offered Wednesdays through Saturdays, but a menu is always available. Reservations accepted.
Open: 11 a.m.-2 p.m. M-F, 4:30-9 p.m. M-S, closed Su
Dress: casual   ◆◆   **MC V**

Did you know?
Hill Floral Products at Richmond grows more roses than any other rose grower in the United States.

EATON

restaurant nominated by Lois Haggard, clerk-treasurer

The Mississinewa Tavern

125 West Harris Street
Eaton, IN 47338
(317) 396-9371

A popular haunt for local folks, the special attractions at the Mississinewa Tavern on Wednesday nights are the tacos and the taco salad, according to Clerk-Treasurer Haggard. Sorry, no reservations.
Open: 7:30 a.m.-midnight M-Th, 7:30 a.m.-1:30 a.m. F-S, noon-8 p.m. Su
Dress: very casual　　　　❖

FARMLAND

restaurants nominated by Bernice Herndon, deputy clerk-treasurer

Reminisce-A-Bit

101 North Main Street
Farmland, IN 47340
(317) 468-8934

Deputy Clerk-Treasurer Herndon likes the decorative reminders of a bygone era which grace the interior of Reminisce-A-Bit, especially the marble-top soda fountain. Let an old-fashioned ice cream soda or phosphate, or one of the 30 flavors of milk shakes, take you back to yesteryear. Reservations accepted.
Open: 10 a.m.-8 p.m. M-S, closed Su
Dress: very casual　　　　❖

The Greene Apple

103 North Main Street
Farmland, IN 47340
(317) 468-8318

Farmland is about 12 miles east of Muncie, at the intersection of SR 32 and SR 1.

As its name suggests, the Greene Apple specializes in homemade desserts made with apples. The restaurant is a luncheon favorite with local officials because of the excellent homemade salads, soups and luncheon croissants, as well as the mouth watering desserts. Reservations accepted.
Open: 9:30 a.m.-5 p.m. T-S, closed Su-M
Dress: casual　　　　❖　　　　**MC V**

FORT WAYNE

restaurant nominated by Paul Helmke, mayor

Casa D' Angelo

(south location)
3402 Fairfield Avenue
Fort Wayne, IN 46807
(219) 745-7200

Casa D' Angelo was started by a former FBI agent and his
partner. The restaurant is known for its authentic Italian food and
a locally famous house salad. The salad comes already tossed in
the special dressing, but don't ask—the recipe is a closely
guarded secret. Reservations (weekdays only) advised.

Open: 11 a.m.-10 p.m. M-Th, 11 a.m.-11 p.m. F-S, closed Su
Dress: casual/dressy ❖❖❖ **MC V AmEx CB DI DC**

GARRETT

T.G.'s Family Restaurant

1346 South Randolph
Garrett, IN 46738
(219) 357-4489

Quality service and down-home food is what you'll find at
T.G.'s Family Restaurant. The chicken Mennonite and lemon
pepper chicken both come highly rated. Kids can choose from
several delicious-sounding items on the children's menu. Reservations accepted.

Open: 11 a.m.-1:15 p.m T-F, 4:15-7 p.m. T-Th; 4:15-8 p.m. F-S,
10:15 a.m.-1:45 p.m. Su
Dress: casual ❖❖

Railroad Inn

104 North Peters Street
Garrett, IN 46738
(219) 357-5756

If you love trains, don't miss the Railroad Inn where you can dine
amid railroad memorabilia. Once on board, try the broiled cod
and orange roughy. The prime rib and broasted chicken are
highly rated, too. Reservations advised.

Open: 7 a.m.-11 p.m. M-S, 8 a.m.-9 p.m. Su
Dress: casual ❖❖ **MC V**

HAGERSTOWN

Welliver's
★ See Top Ten list, page 3 ★

HARLAN

restaurant nominated by David McComb, councilmember, Huntertown

Around the Corner Restaurant

11911 Water Street
Harlan, IN 46743
(219) 657-8058

Exit SR 469 at SR 37, go north 6 miles to Harlan, turn left at Water St.

Come around the corner to Harlan and enjoy some country elegance in a warm, friendly atmosphere. You're just minutes from Fort Wayne, but Around the Corner seems like another world—away from the hustle and bustle. Enjoy a variety of menu choices and daily specials. Sorry, no reservations.
Open: 11 a.m.-9 p.m. T-F, 4 p.m.-9 p.m. S, closed Su-M
Dress: casual/dressy   ◆◆/◆◆◆

HUNTINGTON

restaurant nominated by Gene Snowden, mayor

Nick's Kitchen

506 North Jefferson Street
Huntington, IN 46750
(219) 356-6618

Mayor Snowden says Nick's Kitchen is probably the only place in the world where you can enjoy a "Quayle" hamburger. Former U.S. Senator from Indiana Dan Quayle launched his successful campaign for U.S. Vice President from Nick's Kitchen, Huntington's oldest restaurant. Sorry, no reservations.
Open: 5:30 a.m.-2 p.m. M-S, closed Su
Dress: very casual   ◆

restaurant nominated by Melba Edwards, clerk-treasurer, Zanesville

Richard's Family Restaurant

2865 Guilford Street
Huntington, IN 46750
(219) 356-2964

A great place for family dining due to reasonable prices and the

extensive children's menu, Richard's is a favorite of Zanesville
Clerk-Treasurer Edwards, who recommends the pot roast, apple
dumplings and chicken dishes.
Open: 6 a.m.-9 p.m. M-Th, 6 a.m.-10 p.m. F-S, 7 a.m.-9 p.m. Su
Dress: very casual   ❖

MARION

Yesterday's Diner

3015 South Washington
Marion, IN 46953
(317) 664-2233

Come enjoy the 1950s style decor and the unique pies at
Yesterday's Diner. Choose from an assortment of sandwiches like
The King (a giant hand-breaded tenderloin), or the Patty Duke
(a quarter-pound hamburger). Reservations accepted.
Open: 6 a.m.-8 p.m. M-S, closed Su
Dress: very casual   ❖

MONTPELIER

Grandma Jo's

State Road 18 West
Montpelier, IN 47359
(317) 728-5444

*Grandma Jo's is
on the west edge
of Montpelier on
SR 18.*

You'll feel like you're at grandma's when you enter this popular
eatery. Here the local folks report they serve "some of the finest
breaded tenderloins around." The lasagna and potato salad are
popular selections, too, and the all-you-can-eat fish on Fridays
gets rave reviews. Reservations accepted.
Open: 6 a.m.-8 p.m. M-F, 7 a.m.-3 p.m. S-Su
Dress: very casual   ❖❖

Frosty's

659 West Huntington Street
Montpelier, IN 47539
(317) 728-2257

One of the oldest restaurants in Montpelier, Frosty's features a
highly recommended taco salad with hot sauce and sour cream.
The Frosty burgers are good, too. Reservations accepted.
Open: 11 a.m.-9 p.m. daily
Dress: very casual   **45**

MUNCIE
restaurant nominated by David M. Dominick, mayor

Vince's Restaurant

5301 North Walnut
Muncie, IN 47302
(317) 284-6364

From I-69 take SR 332 East to Walnut, then go north 1..5 miles.

Vince's, a Muncie tradition since 1981, offers diners casual surroundings, great food and outstanding service. Try the hickory smoked chicken and ribs or the slow roasted prime rib. You haven't been to Muncie until you've been to Vince's. Reservations accepted.

Open: 11 a.m.-10 p.m. M-F, 7 a.m.-10 p.m. S-Su
Dress: casual   ❖❖   **MC V AmEx CB DI DC**

NORTH MANCHESTER
restaurants nominated by Nancy Reed, clerk-treasurer

The Hospitality House

202 North Walnut Street
North Manchester, IN 46962
(219) 982-6229

Take SR 114 to downtown North Manchester, turn on Walnut and go 1 block to a Victorian Inn.

Located in the Old Sheller Hotel, The Hospitality House continues Jane Sheller's tradition of old-fashioned hospitality. Open for breakfast and lunch, the Hospitality House features daily specials and unique sandwiches, salads and entrees named after well-known guests at the hotel. Clerk-Treasurer Reed recommends the fresh-baked dinner rolls. Reservations accepted.

Open: 7:30 a.m.-2 p.m. T-S, 10:30 a.m.-1:30 p.m. Su, closed M
Dress: casual   ❖❖   **MC V**

The Main View

141 East Main Street
North Manchester, IN 46962
(219) 982-9900

On Main Street, of course, The Main View entices visitors into its dining area with a warm atmosphere created by historic decor. Clerk-Treasurer Reed raves about the steaks and soups. Reservations accepted for banquet room only.

Open: 11 a.m.-11 p.m. M-S, closed Su
Dress: casual   ❖❖

Mr. Dave's Resturant

102 East Main Street
North Manchester, IN 48962
(219) 982-4769

People drive out of their way for one of Mr. Dave's award-winning fresh pork sandwiches. The hand-breaded pork tenderloin is his specialty—you can order one grilled or fried. Once you've tasted one of his special tenderloins, arrange to have some sent to you, frozen. They ship all over the country. Sorry, no reservations.
Open: 8 a.m.-8 p.m. M-S, closed Su
Dress: casual   ❖

PENDLETON

*restaurants nominated by Loueva Hagemier, councilmember,
and Bart Holleffield, councilmember*

Downing's Old Trail Restaurant

114 North Pendleton Avenue
Pendleton, IN 46064
(317) 778-7595

1/2 block north of the stoplight in downtown Pendleton.

Family owned since 1945, Downing's Old Trail Restaurant draws customers from far and wide. The broasted chicken dinner and the barbecued ribs both receive high praise from Pendleton officials. Reservations accepted.
Open: 11 a.m.-11 p.m. T-Th, 11 a.m.-10 p.m. F-S,
11 a.m.-7 p.m. Su, closed M
Dress: casual   ❖❖   **MC V AmEx Di**

Jimmie's Dairy Bar

7065 State Road 67 South
Pendleton, IN 46064
(317) 778-3800

Jimmie's Dairy Bar has served local residents since 1954. Not only is Jimmie's known for some of the best barbecue in Indiana, their other specialties like homemade coney sauce on quarter-pound hot dogs, upside-down banana splits, and homemade tangerine ice cream are favorites. Sorry, no reservations.
Open: 10:30 a.m.-10 p.m. Su-Th, 10:30 a.m.-11 p.m. F-S
Dress: very casual   ❖

The Pendleton House

118 North Pendleton Avenue
Pendleton, IN 46064
(317) 778-8061

You'll find fresh products prepared wholesomely at The Pendleton House. Relax and enjoy the beautiful Victorian decor throughout the intimate rooms while you dine on eclectic continental cuisine. Lunch favorites include olive nut cream cheese sandwiches. For dinner, try the beef Wellington. Reservations advised.

Open: 11 a.m.-2:30 p.m. M-S, 6-9 p.m. F-S, closed Su
Dress: casual/dressy　　　　　　❖❖　　　　　　　　　**MC V**

The Post Restaurant

Corner of state roads 67 & 9
Pendleton, IN 46064
(317) 778-4651

Take Exit 19 from I-69 into Pendleton, turn right at the first stop light and follow road to SR 67 and SR 9.

"Good home cooking and a friendly atmosphere" complement an excellent menu at The Post Restaurant. During growing season, locally grown organic vegetables and fruits are used. For a treat, try the Russian cabbage soup or the German potato soup with dumplings. The best tip:`don't miss the homemade pies. Reservations accepted.

Open: 5 a.m.-8 p.m. M-S, 5 a.m.-3 p.m. Su
Dress: very casual　　　　　　❖❖

PERU

restaurants nominated by David Livengood, mayor

The Siding

8 West Tenth Street
Peru, IN 46970
(317) 473-4041

Dine in a 1937 railroad car at The Siding, while you enjoy the beautiful historic railroad decor. Mayor Livengood recommends that you try the prime rib. The buffet is a popular choice, too. Reservations accepted.

Open: 11 a.m.-2 p.m. T-F, 4:30-9 p.m. T-S, closed Su-M
Dress: casual　　　　　　❖❖　　　　　　　　　**MC AmEx**

Grant Street Bar & Grill

26 Grant Street
Peru, IN 46970
(317) 472-3997

Each plate at Grant Street Bar & Grill is individually prepared with a French/California flair.

Mayor Livengood proclaims the Grant Street Bar & Grill has one of the "world's greatest" chefs behind the oven, and that there isn't a bad selection on the menu. Try the pan roasted filet of beef with a brandy mushroom cream sauce, or the chicken breast stuffed with spinach and feta cheese. Reservations advised.

**Open: 11 a.m.-2:30 p.m. T-S, 5:30-9:30 p.m. F-S,
11 a.m.-2 p.m. Su**
Dress: casual ❖❖❖ **MC V**

RICHMOND

restaurants nominated by Geneva Allen, councilmember

Bud King's Taste of the Town

1616 East Main Street
Richmond, IN 47374
(317) 935-5464

Homemade soups and live entertainment at Taste of the Town are what appeal to Councilmember Allen. Try the prime rib, shrimp tempura or baked ham loaf, and don't miss the homemade desserts. The Pecan Ball, vanilla ice cream smothered in pecans and carmel sauce, defies description. Reservations accepted.

Open: 11 a.m.-10 p.m. M-F, 4 p.m.-10 p.m. S, closed Su
Dress: casual/dressy ❖❖❖ **MC V AmEx DI**

Connie's

1500 North "E" Street
Richmond, IN 47374
(317) 966-2016

Connie's is "where friends meet" for excellent Greek cuisine, or a variety of steaks, chops, seafood, and chicken. The Greek salad is locally famous, and you won't want to miss trying the delicious baklava for dessert. Reservations advised.

**Open: 11 a.m.-11 p.m. M-Th, 11 a.m.-midnight F,
3 p.m.-midnight S, closed Su**
Dress: casual/dressy ❖❖❖ **MC V AmEx DI**

> *Did you know?*
> The smallest city in Indiana is Woodburn, pop.
> 1,002. It lies 15 miles east of Fort Wayne.

EASTERN

The Olde Richmond Inn

138 South Fifth Street
Richmond, IN 47374
(317) 962-0247

The art of saute cooking is alive and well at the Olde Richmond Inn where you'll want to try the shrimp bianca. It's the chef's secret recipe—jumbo shrimp sauteed in white wine and lightly seasoned with garlic. Relax in Victorian charm while you enjoy mouth watering specials. Reservations advised.
**Open: 11 a.m.-9 p.m. M-Th, 11 a.m.-10 p.m. F-S,
11 a.m.-8 p.m. Su**
Dress: dressy ❖❖/❖❖❖ **MC V**

RUSHVILLE
restaurants nominated by John McCane, mayor

Miller's Family Restaurant & Drive-In

303 South Main Street
Rushville, IN 46173
(317) 938-1234
Drive-In—301 South Main Street
(317) 932-3062

Excellent broasted chicken, tenderloins, and mouth-watering prime rib are the local favorites at this Rushville institution, a frequent site of group functions including regional meetings of mayors and other municipal officials. Reservations accepted for restaurant only.
**Restaurant open: 4:30 - 9 p.m. T-W, 11 a.m.-10 p.m. Th-Su
(summer hours may vary)**
**Drive-In open: 10:30 a.m.-11 p.m. T-Th, Su;
10:30 a.m.-midnight F-S
both closed M**
Dress: casual ❖❖ **MC AmEx CB DI CD**
(restaurant only)

Pizza King

211 North Perkins Street
Rushville, IN 46173
(317) 932-2212

This Pizza King is the only restaurant in Indiana where the mayor of the city will serve your meal. Rushville's affable Mayor McCane proclaims "all the food is great," but his recommendation is the Royal Feast Pizza with mountains of meats and vegetables sufficient to satisfy any citizen's culinary concerns.

Reservations accepted.
Open: 11 a.m.-11 p.m. Su-Th, 11 a.m.-1 a.m. F-S
Dress: casual ❖

Kuch's Kove

102 South Main Street
Sweetser, IN 46987
(317) 384-7820

A family owned and operated restaurant and bar, Kuch's Kove is a favorite of many area residents because of the relaxing atmosphere and good food. Favorites include the Kuch burger, Mary's special hand-breaded tenderloin, or any of the hand-cut steaks. Sorry, no reservations.
Open: 10 a.m.-1:30 p.m., 4:30 p.m.-10 p.m. M-S, closed Su
Dress: casual ❖❖❖

Faye's Northside

506 North Main
Tipton, IN 46072
(317) 675-4191

This is the place where folks like to go to talk about whatever is on their minds, while dining on reasonably priced delicious food. Try the beef and noodles or chicken dumplings, and don't forget the homemade pie! Reservations accepted.
Open: 5 a.m.-3 p.m. M-F, 5-10:30 a.m. S, closed Su
Dress: casual ❖❖

> *Did you know?*
> Indiana's most unusual newspaper—by modern standards at least—wsa the *Dog Fennel Gazette* of Rushville, circa 1819. It was printed on one side of a page and sent to subscribers who read it, then sent it back to the publisher so he could print the following edition on the back page.

Jim Dandy Family Restaurant

203 West Jefferson
Tipton, IN 46072
(317) 675-6199

The homemade cole slaw, hand-breaded tenderloin and excellent pies are the recommendations at Jim Dandy's, where our scouts report the best in good food, a great salad bar and friendly staff. Reservations accepted for large groups only.
Open: 6 a.m.-10 p.m. M-F, 7 a.m.-10 p.m. S-Su
Dress: casual   ❖   **MC V**

Exit U.S. 31 at SR 28 and go west 4 miles. Jim Dandy is on the south side of the street, one block from downtown.

Sherrill's Restaurant

State Road 28 and U.S. 31
Tipton, IN 46072
(317) 675-3550

Great home-cooked meals at reasonable prices are what makes Sherrill's popular, according to local officials. The homemade noodles and breaded tenderloins are delicious, and the daily specials are the toast of the town. Sorry, no reservations.
Open: 6 a.m.-8 p.m. M-S, 8 a.m.-7 p.m. Su
Dress: very casual   ❖

UNION CITY

Cheryl's Restaurant

415 West Chestnut
Union City, IN 47390
(317) 964-3488

You'll have a lot of time on your hands at Cheryl's because its choice location in this Indiana/Ohio border community leaves it observing two time zones. Try the country breakfast, then stick around for lunch either on Indiana or Ohio time. If you're really hungry, eat twice! While you're eating, you can learn about the local businesses from advertisements adorning the walls. Reservations accepted.
Open: 5 a.m.-3 p.m. M-F, 5 a.m.-2 p.m. S, closed Su
Dress: very casual   ❖

Shadows Restaurant & Cocktail Lounge

State Road 28
Union City, IN 47390
(317) 964-5555

Located on SR 28 at the western edge of Union City.

Bring your appetite to Shadows Restaurant & Lounge, where the featured attractions include the homemade pies, breads, and the barbecued ribs. The sumptuous salad bar is recommended, too. Reservations accepted for the party room only.
Open: 11 a.m.-midnight M-F, 11 a.m.-1 a.m. S, closed Su except Easter and Mother's Day
Dress: casual   ❖❖   **MC V**

UPLAND

Ivanhoe's

914 South Main Street
Upland, IN 46989
(317) 998-7261

With 100 shakes and 100 sundaes on the menu at Ivanhoe's, you're sure to find something to delight your tastebuds. Oh, they have delicious sandwiches and salads, too. Sorry no reservations.
Open: 11 a.m.-10 p.m. M-Th, 11 a.m.-11 p.m. F-S, 2-10 p.m. Su
Dress: very casual   ❖

WABASH

Eugenia's at the Honeywell Center

275 West Market Street
Wabash, IN 46992
(219) 563-4411

Eugenia's offers elegant dining at casual prices. Located at the Honeywell Center, site of art exhibits and a theater, Eugenia's is convenient for lunch or Sunday brunch. Or, call ahead for theater tickets and dine at the pre-concert buffet. Reservations advised.
Open: 11 a.m.-2 p.m. daily, 4-9 p.m. F-S,
6-9 p.m. for concert events
Dress: casual   ❖❖/❖❖❖   **MC V**

Mike's Little Italy

1012 North Cass Street
Wabash, IN 46992
(219) 563-1982

Mike's Little Italy is about 1/8 mile south of SR 24 on SR 15.

If Italian food is what you crave, Mike's Little Italy is one of the oldest and finest restaurants in Wabash. Mike's serves up some of the best lasagna and spaghetti in Indiana, and offers delicious prime rib, too. Reservations accepted.

Open: 11 a.m.-11 p.m. M-S, closed Su
Dress: very casual ❖❖ **MC V**

Did you know?
The first Indiana city to have electric street lighting was Wabash, which switched to the system in 1880.

Monumental marvels, sports, shopping features of heartland

From fascinating museums to history-making sports, central Indiana boasts a treasure trove of enticing attractions. The shadows of the glass and steel skyscrapers of downtown Indianapolis fall gracefully on quaint neighborhoods, woods, lakes, and parks. Nearby is Lockerbie Square, a restored 19th century downtown residential area where Hoosier poet James Whitcomb Riley once penned his rhymes. Venture a little farther to discover charming towns, like Greenfield and Noblesville, which have recently revitalized their historical city squares and neighborhoods.

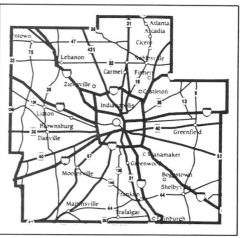

Indianapolis, considered the Amateur Sports Capital of the World, has hosted such sporting events as the NCAA Final Four, NCAA swimming and diving championships, U.S. Rowing nationals, track and field championships, and the 1987 Pan American Games. Also, Indianapolis is home to the Indianapolis Colts, Indiana Pacers, Indianapolis Indians, and the Indianapolis Ice. Speedway holds its own claim to fame with the Indianapolis Motor Speedway, home of the Indianapolis 500, the Brickyard 400, and the Speedway Museum.

In terms of history, the heartland is home to such monumental structures as the Indiana Soldiers' & Sailors' Monument and the nation's first Union Station. This union railway depot, where Thomas Edison once was a Western Union telegraph operator, has been renovated into a festival marketplace featuring express eateries, seven full-service restaurants, four night clubs and more than 45 specialty shops.

Take a little detour north of Indianapolis to Fishers, where one of the nation's finest living history museums, Conner Prairie, an 1830s pioneer village and prairie settlement, stands. Down the road, quaint shops, fine art and country crafts line the brick streets of Zionsville. And in Carmel, where, according to legend, the first electric traffic signal in the United States was installed in 1923, explore the Museum of Miniature Houses.

Head east to Greenfield to see the Old Log Jail and many sites honoring native son James Whitcomb Riley. The once radical design of the Boone County Courthouse is worth the trip to Lebanon, where you can explore the Flower Barn, an everlasting flower farm.

To the south, the Horizons Outlet Center in Edinburgh is worth the short trip on I-65.

You might consider taking a tour of the 1894 Rock House in Morgantown, a turreted, gabled Victorian structure embedded with shards of pottery, bits of jewelry, doorknobs, seashells, Indian relics, and old photographs. It is now a 13-room bed and breakfast.

Feeling weighed down? Take a quick trip to Gravity Hill in Mooresville. Stop your car at the bottom; put it in neutral and watch what happens—you'll coast *up* the hill for almost a quarter of a mile. According to local legend, the phenomena is a result of the power of an Indian witch doctor buried at the foot of the hill.

And, if shopping is what you want, get ready to charge—this amateur sports capital of the world also claims some Olympic-level shopping. Circle Centre mall, the crown jewel of Indianapolis' nationally lauded downtown revitalization, opens in Fall 1995. This shopping arena will occupy four city blocks and include anchor department stores Nordstrom and Parisian, about 100 specialty stores, and theme restaurants, nightclubs and a 12-screen cinema.

These are only a few of *many* exciting and interesting things that await you in the Hoosier Heartland. For more information, contact the local visitors bureaus listed below:

Indianapolis...............(317) 237-5200 or 1-800-323-4639

Hamilton County.........(317) 237-5200 or 1-800-776-8687

Zionsville...(317) 873-3836

Boone County/Lebanon...........................(317) 482-1320

Fishers...(317) 578-0700

Greenfield...(317) 462-4188

Greenwood...(317) 888-4856

Greater Martinsville.................................(317) 342-8110

Mooresville...(317) 831-6509

Shelby County..(317) 398-6647

Fletcher's of Atlanta

185 West Main Street
Atlanta, IN 46031
(317) 292-2777

Go 5 miles east of U.S. 31 on Hamilton/Tipton County Line Rd., then 1 1/2 blocks south on Walnut.

You can drive to Fletcher's, or every-other week (seasonally) take a relaxing train excursion from Fishers to Atlanta via the Hamiltonian. Once there, enjoy a variety of tempting entrees made from locally grown products. Popular entrees include the Hunan barbecued rack of lamb, and Hog Heaven, bourbon-onion marinated pork chops. Reservations advised.

Open: 5-9 p.m. T-F, 5-10 p.m. S, closed Su-M
Dress: casual   ◆◆◆◆   **MC V CB DC**

BEECH GROVE

restaurants nominated by Warner Wiley, mayor

Chan's Garden Restaurant

718 Main Street
Beech Grove, IN 46107
(317) 788-0601

Take Beech Grove exit from I-65 and turn north to Main St.

If authentic Chinese food is what you're hungry for, try Chan's Garden. The owners will serve up a meal to satisfy any craving for *real* Chinese food. Mayor Wiley's favorite dish is the chicken fried rice. The cashew chicken or Cantonese chicken chow mein or lo mein are good, too. Reservations advised.

Open: 11 a.m.-9 p.m. M-F, 11 a.m.-9:30 p.m. S,
11 a.m.-7:30 p.m. Su
Dress: casual   ◆◆   **MC V AmEx**

Napoli Villa Restaurant

758 Main Street
Beech Grove, IN 46107
(317) 783-4122

Stop two on the ethnic dining tour of Beech Grove is another family owned/operated eatery, the Napoli Villa, where Mayor Wiley recommends you try the fresh baked goods and delicious dessert after a sumptuous spaghetti dinner. Reservations advised.

Open: 11 a.m.-2 p.m., 5-9:30 p.m. M-Th; 5-10:30 p.m. F-S,
closed Su
Dress: casual   ◆/◆◆◆   **MC V AmEx CB DC**

CENTRAL

BOGGSTOWN

restaurant nominated by Bob Williams, mayor, Shelbyville

Boggstown Inn and Cabaret

6895 West Boggstown Road
Boggstown, IN 46176
(317) 835-2020

8 1/2 miles from I-74 in Shelby County.

The Boggstown Inn and Cabaret is a favorite of Shelbyville Mayor Williams who enjoys the ragtime music, singing, and other entertainment provided as part of the dinner package at the popular Shelby County spot. The mayor's favorite is the prime rib. Dinner by reservation only.

Open: depends on number of reservations, call first
Dress: casual   ◆◆◆   **MC V**

CARMEL

Cancun Mexican Restaurant & Cantina

511 South Rangeline Road
Carmel, IN 46032
(317) 580-0333

Newly opened in 1994, the Cancun rapidly amassed a large following of Mexican cuisine lovers in and around northern Indianapolis suburban communities. Try the fajitas or combination dinner while you enjoy the strolling guitarist who serenades weekend diners. Reservations accepted.

Open: 11 a.m.-10 p.m. M-F, noon-10:30 p.m. S-Su
Dress: casual   ◆◆   **MC V AmEx**

Helio's Tea Room

220 East Main Street
Carmel, IN 46032
(317) 844-4606

Local folks suggest the luncheon soup special and dessert of the day at this newly decorated tea room. Then, drop by the delightful gift shop. Helio's offers low-fat lunches and low-fat desserts, too. Reservations advised.

Open: 11 a.m.-2 p.m. M-S, closed Su
Dress: casual   ◆◆   **MC V**

> *Did you know?*
> The first electronic traffic light is believed to have been installed in 1923 in Carmel.

Ice Creams Coffee Beans Cafe

1404 South Rangeline Road
Carmel, IN 46032
(317) 844-8643

Located at the northwest corner of 116th St. and Rangeline Rd., in The Centre, next to Osco Drugs.

Local officials like to brag about the creative menu at Ice Creams Coffee Beans Cafe, featuring unusual specialty sandwiches including the chicken salad club sandwich, voted the "best" in the greater Indianapolis area in 1994. Or try one of their famous pound-and-a-half baked potatoes. Sorry, no reservations.
Open: 10 a.m.-9 p.m. M-S, closed Su
Dress: casual   ◆◆

DANVILLE

restaurants nominated by Pauletta Frye, clerk-treasurer

J.J.'s Bar and Restaurant

28 West Main Street
Danville, IN 46122
(317) 745-7444

If you crave a friendly, hometown atmosphere along with some delicious food, try J.J.'s Bar and Restaurant. Located in one of the original buildings from when Danville was laid out, J.J.'s offers a bit of Americana in the painted "Mail Pouch Tobacco" advertisement on the building's west side. Try the stuffed Italian roast beef special, the New York strip steak, or a number of Mexican specialties. Reservations accepted.
Open: 8 a.m.-midnight M-F, 9 a.m.-midnight S, 4 p.m.-midnight Su
Dress: very casual   ◆   MC V

Mayberry Cafe

78 West Main Street
Danville, IN 46122
(317) 745-4067

Tuesday night is "Goober's Hat Night." Any customer wearing a hat gets a free dessert with the purchase of any dinner.

If Barney Fife was the deputy sheriff in Danville, he'd eat at the Mayberry Cafe, where the decor and menu are a tribute to the popular Andy Griffith Show television series starring Andy Griffith and Don Knotts. Food's good too, according to Clerk-Treasurer Frye. Sorry, no reservations.
Open: 11 a.m.-2 p.m. M-S, 4:30-9 p.m. Tu-S, 11 a.m.-8 p.m. Su
Dress: very casual   ◆/◆◆

CENTRAL

59

EDINBURGH

restaurant nominated by Ken Banta, councilmember

Schaffers Old Towne Inn & Museum

107 East Main Cross Street
Edinburgh, IN 46124
(812) 526-0275

Fine dining and attractive antiques go together at Schaffers according to Councilmember Banta, who claims the downtown establishment is the most complete antique pharmacy museum in the Midwest. He recommends you try the prime rib. Reservations accepted.

Open: 10:30 a.m.-2 p.m. M-W, 10:30 a.m.-8 p.m. Th, 10:30 a.m.-9 p.m. F-S, closed Su
Dress: casual ❖❖❖ **MC V AmEx**

FISHERS

restaurants nominated by Walter Kelly, councilmember

Governor Noble's Eating Place

13400 Allisonville Road, Conner Prairie
Fishers, IN 46038
(317) 776-6008

Besides a lifelike look into Indiana's past, Conner Prairie offers visitors a chance to delight in homestyle food and genuine Hoosier hospitality at Governor Noble's Eating Place. Conner Prairie village tours and special programs are available. Reservations accepted.

Open: 11:30 a.m.-2:30 p.m. T-S, 11 a.m.-2 p.m. Su, closed M
Dress: casual ❖❖ **MC V AmEx DI**

Nickel Plate Bar & Grill

8654 East 116th Street
Fishers, IN 46038
(317) 841-2888

Relax and enjoy the informal dining at this quaint local pub along the historic Nickel Plate Railroad. The Nickel Plate Bar & Grill is recognized for its giant-sized tenderloin and creative burgers. Experience great food and service in a comfortable and friendly atmosphere. Councilmember Kelley recommends you try the "Monon hamburger." Reservations accepted.

Open: 11 a.m.-11 p.m. M-Th, 11 a.m.-midnight F-S, noon-8 p.m. Su
Dress: casual ❖❖ **MC V AmEx DI**

Heiskell's Restaurant & Lounge

398 South Main Street
Franklin, IN 46131
(317) 736-4900

Heiskell's is in a home built at the turn of the century by Walter W. Aikens, founder and publisher of the Franklin Evening Star newspaper.

A turn-of-the-century Greek-revival mansion houses Heiskell's, where diners can enjoy terrific food and a unique atmosphere. The observant diner will notice the original gas and electric light fixtures, leaded and stained glass windows, original Tiffany lamps, and hardwood floors. Try the herb-crusted prime rib, and the home-baked pies, cakes and pastries. Reservations advised.

Open: 11:30 a.m.-2 p.m., 5:30-9 p.m. W-F; 5:30-9 p.m. S, closed Su-Tu
Dress: casual/dressy   ❖❖❖   **MC V AmEx CB DI DC**

GREENFIELD

restaurants nominated by Keith J. McClarnon, mayor

Brandywine Steak House

20 West Main Street
Greenfield, IN 46140
(317) 462-4466

Brandywine is proud of its loyal staff—many of whom have been here a quarter-century or more—enhancing your dining pleasure. Mayor McClarnon favors the fillet mignon and the wide variety of seafood dishes. Reservations accepted.

Open: 4:30-9:30 p.m. M-Th, 4:30-10:30 p.m. F-S, closed Su
Dress: casual   ❖❖❖   **MC V AmEx DI DC**

Dragon Palace

413 North State Street
Greenfield, IN 46140
(317) 462-4965

Located 3 blocks from the hospital on SR 9.

The first Oriental restaurant in Greenfield, Dragon Palace offers a delicious lunch buffet. Also popular is General Tao's chicken. Mayor McClarnon reports the wonton soup and egg rolls "are tops." Reservations accepted.

Open: 11 a.m.-9 p.m. M-F, 11:30 a.m.-9:30 p.m. S,
11:30 a.m.-8 p.m. Su
Dress: casual   ❖❖   **MC V**

Patricia's Chocolate

14 West Main Street
Greenfield, IN 46140
(317) 462-5244

"A touch of Europe on the historic Greenfield city square" is what locals call the delightful Patricia's Chocolate restaurant and candy store. Menu specialities include the vegetarian lasagna and turtle pie. A variety of European coffees are available. Pick up a box of the homemade chocolates on your way out. Sorry, no reservations.
Open: 10 a.m.-4:30 p.m. M-F, 11:30 a.m.-4:30 p.m. F-S, closed Su
Dress: casual   ❖

GREENWOOD

Haus Anna

67 North Madison Avenue
Greenwood, IN 46142
(317) 887-0439

Located 3 blocks north of Main St. on the east side of Madison Ave.

Absorb the authentic gasthaus atmosphere of Haus Anna, where with just six employees they make some of the best German food around, including authentic schnitzel and sauerbraten. An outstanding evening smorgasbord and a limited menu are available daily. Reservations accepted for groups of 8 or more.
Open: 11 a.m.-2 p.m., 4 p.m.-9p.m. T-Th; 11 a.m.-2 p.m.,
4 p.m.-10 p.m. F; 11 a.m.-10 p.m. S; 11 a.m.-2 p.m. Su
Dress: casual   ❖❖❖

Johnson County Line

1265 North Madison Avenue
Greenwood, IN 46142
(317) 887-0404

For excellent prime rib, seafood and steaks, head for Johnson County Line where all entrees are made fresh and in-house. Frequent wine tastings feature well-known personalities from the wine industry. Reservations advised.
Open: 5-9 p.m. Su-Th, 5-10 p.m. F-S
Dress: casual   ❖❖❖   **MC V AmEx CB DC**

restaurant nominated by Mary T. Cook, clerk-treasurer, McCordsville

The Blue Heron

11699 Fall Creek Road
Indianapolis, IN 46256
(317) 845-8899

Take 96th St. east to Fall Creek Rd., turn left and go 2 miles.

This lakeside haven on the far Northeast side of Indianapolis serves the best in steaks and fresh seafood. Clerk-Treasurer Cook recommends the seafood fettuccine; the tomato basil pasta is good, too. Reservations advised.
Open: 11 a.m.-midnight M-S, 9 a.m.-11 p.m. Su
Dress: casual   ❖❖❖   **MC V AmEx CB Di DC**

restaurant nominated by Dr. Philip C. Borst, councilmember

Fireside South Restaurant

522 East Raymond Street
Indianapolis, IN 46203
(317) 788-4521

Steaks served at your table on sizzling platters are the favorite of Councilmember Borst at the Fireside, family owned and operated for nearly 50 years. German dishes, too, are a specialty of the house. The Fireside has several private dining areas and is a popular choice for group parties. Reservations advised.
Open: 11 a.m.-10 p.m. M-Th, 11 a.m.-11 p.m. F, 4-11 p.m. S,
closed Su
Dress: casual   ❖/❖❖❖❖   **MC V AmEx Di**

CENTRAL

> *Did you know?*
> The largest city park in Indiana is Eagle Creek Park in Indianapolis. The park has 1,500 acres of water and 3,500 acres of land. Eagle Creek also is the largest developed municipal park in the United States.

Indianapolis City Market

222 East Market Street
Indianapolis, IN 46204
(317) 634-9266

Indianapolis City Market, directly north of the City-County Building, is a National Historic Landmark.

The only difficulty you may encounter at the historic City Market is deciding where to start to "shop" for lunch. As you enter, note the enticing mix of aromas flowing from numerous lunch stands, produce stalls and exotic spice and imported food shops. Built in 1886, the Market offers guests a choice of Greek, Kosher, Middle Eastern, oriental, and Italian cuisine. Arts and crafts and a variety of other goods are also on sale, and you can enjoy a variety of over 200 special events every year.

Open: 6 a.m.-6 p.m. M-S, closed Su
Dress: very casual ❖

restaurant nominated by Linda Beadling, councilmember

The Iron Skillet

2489 West 30th Street
Indianapolis, IN 46204
(317) 923-6353

A favorite of Councilmember Beadling, The Iron Skillet is located in a century-old home and has been family owned/operated since 1956. Examples of the traditional Hoosier cooking served family style at The Iron Skillet include the fried chicken, walleyed pike, fresh-baked fish, and steaks. Reservations advised.

Open: 5-8:30 p.m. W-S, noon-7:30 p.m. Su, closed M-T
Dress: casual ❖❖❖ MC V AmEx Di DC

St. Elmo Steak House
★ See Top Ten list, page 2 ★

CENTRAL

Did you know?
The largest expense for most municipalities over 5,000 people is police and fire protection. The next most-expensive items are streets and parks.

LEBANON

restaurant nominated by Jim Acton, mayor

The Old Trackside Depot

100 South Street
Lebanon, IN 46052
(317) 483-0400

Housed in a former train station built in 1916, The Old
Trackside Depot offers a diverse menu and attentive staff that
make this one of Mayor Acton's choice spots for dinner. His
favorites are the steak and ribs. Reservations accepted.

Open: 11 a.m.-2 p.m., 5-9 p.m. M-S, closed Su
Dress: casual   ❖❖❖   MC V

McCORDSVILLE

restaurant nominated by Mary T. Cook, clerk-treasurer

Casio's Restaurant

6765 Pendleton Pike
McCordsville, IN 46055
(317) 335-2237

Located in a former gambling casino, Casio's is a favorite of
Clerk-Treasurer Cook who recommends the prime rib dinner. If
you ask, the staff will give you a guided tour of the historic old
casino, including the bullet-proof cashier's room. Keep your eyes
open for "the Blue Lady," Casio's ghost who travels in a blue
mist. On weekends, dance to the big band sound of "City Life
Trio." Reservations advised.

Open: 5:30-10 p.m. T-Th, 5:30-11 p.m. F-S,
lounge open 3 p.m.-close T-S, closed Su-M
Dress: casual/dressy   ❖❖❖   MC V DI

MOORESVILLE

Gray Brothers Cafeteria

555 South Indiana
Mooresville, IN 46158
(317) 831-3345

Gray Brothers Cafeteria serves some of the finest food around.
Local officials give this establishment high marks for its variety,
quality and delicious desserts. Sorry, no reservations.

Open: daily, 11 a.m.-9 p.m.
Dress: casual

CENTRAL

MORGANTOWN

restaurant nominated by Lora Ford, clerk-treasurer

Touch of Country Class

249 West Washington Street
Morgantown, IN 46160

*Just west of the
4-way stop at
SR 135 and SR
252, on SR 252.*

A unique combination of antiques and crafts make the Touch of
Country Class a delightful diversion. The chicken salad and
home-cooked Sunday dinners are highly recommended. A
unique blend of coffee and tea is available. Reservations
accepted.

Open: 10 a.m.-5 p.m. M, W-Su; closed Tu
Dress: casual   ❖❖   **MC V DI**

The Vault Cafe

170 West Washington Street
Morgantown, IN 46160

As its name suggests, The Vault Cafe is housed in a former bank
building from the 1800s. Try their one-pound jumbo burritos or
one of the California-style salads, and don't forget to leave room
for a piece of homemade cake or other delectable dessert.
Reservations accepted.

Open: noon-7 p.m. M, Th-Su; closed Tu-W
Dress: casual   ❖

NOBLESVILLE

Lutz's Steak House

3100 Westfield Road
Noblesville, IN 46060

Local officials praise Lutz's for consistently great food since
1976. The prime rib and New York strip steak dinners are
highly recommended, as well as the seafood. Live entertainment
is featured four nights a week. Reservations advised.

Open: 11 a.m.-9:30 p.m. M-Th, 11 a.m.-10:30 p.m. F,
5-10:30 p.m. S, closed Su
Dress: casual   ❖❖❖   **MC V AmEx DC**

PITTSBORO

restaurant nominated by Shirley Riddle, clerk-treasurer

Frank and Mary's

P.O. Box 143,
21-25 East Main Street
Pittsboro, IN 46167
(317) 893-3485

From I-74 take Pittsboro Exit, turn south to Pittsboro, go 1 block east of stoplight on SR 136.

A central Indiana institution for decades and occasional hangout for Indianapolis Motor Speedway celebrities, Frank and Mary's is one of Hoosierland's more famous catfish dinner spots. Clerk-Treasurer Riddle says unequivocally the catfish is "The Best." Reservations accepted for parties of 10 or more.

Open: 11 a.m.-1:30 p.m., 5-10 p.m. M-Th; 11 a.m.-11 p.m. F-S; closed Su
Dress: casual   ❖❖   **MC V**

SHELBYVILLE

restaurant nominated by Bob Williams, mayor

Fiddlers Three

1415 East Michigan Road
Shelbyville, IN 46176
(317) 392-4306

1 mile west of SR 44 Exit off I-74.

Beautiful leaded glass windows enhance the atmosphere at Fiddler's Three, where you'll find top-of-the-line steaks and delicious lunch selections. Mayor Williams' favorite meal is the "Wickersham," open-faced ground beef or chicken breast, sauteed mushrooms and onions, and melted Swiss cheese, served with steak fries and soup or salad. Reservations advised.

Open: 11 a.m.-2 p.m. Tu-F, 5-9 p.m. T-Th, 5-10 p.m. F-S, closed Su-M
Dress: casual   ❖❖   **MC V**

CENTRAL

Did you know?
In 1907 Indianapolis ranked fourth in the nation in auto production; by 1913 it rose to second, but failed to place in the top 10 by 1920.

SHERIDAN

restaurant nominated by Connie Pearson, clerk-treasurer

The Red Onion Restaurant & Lounge

406 South Main Street
Sheridan, IN 46069
(317) 758-0424

Take U.S. 31 north to SR 38, go west to Main St., then 1 1/2 blocks.

Clerk-Treasurer Pearson calls the Red Onion "a place to mellow out with friends." Home-cooked food is the specialty of the house. Enjoy breaded tenderloins, or all-you-can-eat broasted chicken, fish or popcorn shrimp on Tuesdays and Wednesdays. Reservations advised.
Open: 11 a.m.-2 p.m. M-S, 4:30-9 p.m. T-Th, 4:30-10 p.m. F-S, closed Su
Dress: casual   ❖❖❖

SPEEDWAY

restaurant nominated by John Sneyd, clerk-treasurer

Union Jack Pub

6225 West 25th
Speedway, IN 46224
(317) 243-3300

Near the Indianapolis Motor Speedway.

Superb salads and sandwiches are the trademark of Union Jack's, according to Clerk-Treasurer Sneyd, where his favorite is the Chicago-style pizza. If you're an auto racing fan, you'll enjoy the racing memorabilia in this English pub. Sorry, no reservations.
Open: 11 a.m.-11 p.m. M-Th, 11 a.m.-1 a.m. F-S, noon-midnight Su
Dress: very casual   ❖❖   MC V AmEx CB DI DC

THORNTOWN

restaurant nominated by Jim Acton, mayor, Lebanon

Stookey's Restaurant

125 East Main
Thorntown, IN 46071
(317) 436-7202

Racing and basketball highlight the interior of Stookey's, where you'll also find excellent catfish and steaks. Mayor Acton's favorite meal is the ribeye steak. Sorry, no reservations.

Open: 11 a.m.-2 p.m. M-S, 5-9 p.m. T-Th, 5-10 p.m. F-S, closed Su
Dress: casual   ❖❖

TRAFALGAR

Silver Spur Western Dance/Dinner Theater

P.O. Box 96
107 South Pleasant
Trafalgar, IN 46181
(317) 878-4424

From SR 135, turn east at the flashing yellow light (Pearl St.), and go 6 blocks.

Enjoy line dancing and live entertainment along with some of the state's finest home-cooked meals at Silver Spur, where everything is done with a western flair. Reservations advised.
Open: 5-8 p.m. (buffet), 8 p.m.-midnight (dancing) F-S
Dress: casual   ❖❖

Did you know?
The first successful goldfish farm in the
nation was founded at Martinsville in 1899
by Eugene Curtis Shireman with 200 fish.
Today, it still ranks among the biggest
goldfish producers in the world.

Tell us what YOU think!

**Your opinion is very important to us.
Really.**

Please take a few minutes
to write us a note and let us know
what you think of

Indiana's Favorite Hometown Restaurants

Send your comments to
Indiana Association of Cities and Towns
150 West Market Street, Suite 728
Indianapolis, IN 46204

Architecture, art, history await South Central visitors

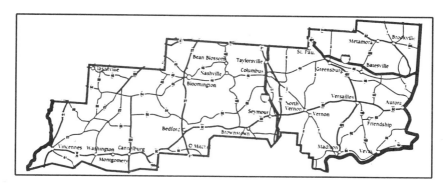

The stunning architectural marvels of Columbus are complemented by the historic pre-statehood structures of Vincennes and stately mansions which hug the Ohio River in this magnificent mid-south region.

No trip to the South Central wonderland is complete without a stop at the Columbus Visitors Center to learn more about this architectural jewel of the prairie. Due to benefactor J. Irwin Miller of Cummins Engine Company, Columbus claims more than 50 public buildings designed by such internationally known architects as I. M. Pei, Eliel and Eero Saarinen and Venturi. After the architectural tour, stop for dessert in downtown Columbus at historic Zaharako's Ice Cream parlor, complete with a 1908 German pipe organ.

The artists colony and shopping mecca of Nashville in scenic Brown County is worth an extended stay. In addition to 350 specialty shops, outstanding restaurants, art galleries, live theater and country music centers, Nashville now has "Elvis." Jasonville Mayor Bruce Borders, who has gained national fame moonlighting as an Elvis impersonator, performs there often.

We'll share a Brown County secret. A hidden jewel for art fanciers is the T. C. Steele State Historic Site, including his home, studio and a large collection of the turn-of-the-century artist's landscapes and portraits. It's nine miles west of Nashville off State Road 46.

Bloomington seems to be populated with people who moved there to attend Indiana University and never went home. Perhaps the allure is such enticements as exotic dining, including the state's only Tibetan Restaurant, diverse live entertainment and a laid back lifestyle that finds farmers, artists, educators, business leaders, and students working and playing side by side. In Bloomington, don't miss the Indiana University Museum of Art and the award-winning

SOUTH CENTRAL

71

Oliver and Butler wineries.

There is more early Indiana history to be retrieved in Vincennes than in any other Hoosier city, including the George Rogers Clark National Historic Park on the Wabash River. The Harrison historical park attractions include the Capitol building for the old Indiana Territory and Grouseland, built in 1803 by Gov. William Henry Harrison, later ninth President of the United States.

History is alive and thriving in the form of more than 100 shops, museums and restaurants in the recreated canal-era village of Metamora, where a shrill steam engine whistle beckons arriving visitors to take a ride on the Whitewater Valley Railroad.

We suggest a one-day, 75-mile auto tour (using scenic state roads 56/156) of Madison, Vevay, Rising Sun, Aurora and Lawrenceburg. The route includes picturesque views of the Ohio River and will guide you to tours of stately homes, antiquing, charming country shops and some of the more intriguing Favorite Hometown Restaurants in Indiana.

There's much more to do and see in this bountiful South Central slice of Hoosierland. For more information, call one of these local visitors bureaus:

Bloomington..............(812) 334-8900 or 1-800-800-0037

Brookville...(317) 647-2177

Columbus...................(812) 378-2622 or 1-800-468-6564

Daviess County...(812) 254-5262

Dearborn County.......................................(812) 537-0814

Linton..(812) 847-4846

Greensburg...(812) 847-4846

Historic Hoosier Hills...............................(812) 689-6456

Jennings County..........(812) 346-4865 or 1-800-928-3667

Lawrence County.......................................(812) 275-7637

Madison...(812) 265-2956

Nashville....................(812) 988-7303 or 1-800-753-3255

Rising Sun...(812) 438-2181

Seymour...(812) 522-3681

Switzerland County.......(812) 427-3237 or 1-800-HELLOW

Vincennes...................(812) 882-6440 or 1-800-886-6443

restaurants nominated by Leon Kelley, mayor

The Coachlight Inn

223 Third Street
Aurora, IN 47001
(812) 926-4006

Family owned and operated, the Coachlight staff prides itself on
its fast, friendly service and the pleasant atmosphere created by
the antique player-piano which tinkles away in the background
for diners. For a treat, try the pot roast over buttered noodles
or the Bar-B-Q baby back ribs. Sorry, no reservations.
Open: 7-10 M-F, 7-11 S-Su
Dress: casual   ❖❖   **MC V**

The Steamboat Clinton

301 Second Street
Aurora, IN 47001
(812) 926-0304

When you dine at the Steamboat Clinton you'll feel as if you're
taking a scenic trip down the nearby Ohio River. The decor has
been modeled after the original Steamboat Clinton which docked
regularly at Aurora more than a century ago. In keeping with the
nautical atmosphere the mayor recommends the seafood platter.
Reservations accepted for large groups.
Open: 11 a.m.-10 p.m. T-Th, 11 a.m.-11p.m. F-S, closed Su-M
Dress: casual   ❖❖/❖❖❖   **MC V**

*To get to Steam-
boat Clinton, follow
SR 56 off Hwy.
50, and go three
blocks.*

Cricket Ridge Public Restaurant/Golf Course

22087 Pocket Road
Batesville, IN 47006
(812) 934-0414

*Take Exit 74 at
SR 229, go
north about 2
miles, then turn
right on Pocket
Road to Cricket
Ridge.*

Play nine holes of golf at Cricket Ridge, then enjoy a meal on
the restaurant deck overlooking the water. The daily luncheon
specials are out of this world—especially the grilled chicken
breast. On Fridays and Saturdays, try the prime rib. Reservations accepted.
**Open: 10:30 a.m.-9 p.m. M-Th, 10:30 a.m.-10 p.m. F-S,
10:30 a.m.-8 p.m. Su**
Dress: casual   ❖❖   **MC V DI**

BLOOMINGTON

restaurants nominated by Tomilea Allison, mayor

Encore Cafe

316 West 6th Street
Bloomington, IN 47404
(812) 333-7312

Encore Cafe is housed in a renovated 1820s warehouse on Bloomington's Historic West Side.

The Encore Cafe is an upscale deli. Mayor Allison says any sandwich you buy here is tasty. She recommends the Big Al sandwich; it's stuffed with roasted peppers, fresh mozzarella and herb vinegar on a bagel. The vegetable chili and spinach lasagna are a vegetarian delight. Sorry, no reservations.
Open: 11 a.m.-11 p.m. M-F, 11 a.m.-1a.m. S-Su
Dress: very casual   ◆◆   **MC   V   AmEx**

Michael's Uptown Cafe & Bakery

102 East Kirkwood
Bloomington, IN 47401
(812) 339-0900

A popular hangout for Bloomingtonians, Michael's Uptown Cafe specializes in some of the best fresh-baked bread and Cajun dishes around including authentic gumbo. The black bean soup is especially delicious. The fresh seafood and the Indonesian chicken kebobs are a real specialty. Reservations accepted.
Open: 7 a.m.-10 p.m. M-F, 8 a.m.-10 p.m. S, 9 a.m.-2 p.m. Su
Dress: casual   ◆/◆◆   **MC   V   AmEx   CB   DI   DC**

The White River Cafe and Coffee Company

910 North College Avenue
Bloomington, IN 47404
(812) 330-1212

The White River Cafe and Coffee Company is splendidly decorated in fabulous Miami (Fla.) art deco. They are known for serving healthy California novelle cuisine. Mayor Allison's favorite meals are the coyote chicken and the fennel pork. They also have an extensive wine list. Reservations accepted.
Open: 11 a.m.-10 p.m. M-Th, 11 a.m.-11 p.m. F,
10 a.m.-11 p.m. S, 10 a.m.-9 p.m. Su
Dress: casual   ◆◆   **MC   V   AmEx   DC**

> *Did you know?*
> Indiana has 115 cities and 460 towns for a total of 575 municipalities.

COLUMBUS

restaurants nominated by Robert Stewart, mayor

The Ribeye Steak and Ribs

2506 25th Street
Columbus, IN 47201
(812) 376-6410

Across from Lincoln Park Ice Skating Rink past Fairoaks Mall.

Mayor Stewart says the fresh cut steaks and a "super" salad bar are what make Ribeye Steak and Ribs a popular gathering spot for local officials and visitors alike. You won't want to miss the fresh-baked bread and cheesecake. Reservations accepted.

Open: 5-9 p.m. M-Th, 5-10 p.m. F-S, 4-8 p.m. Su
Dress: casual ❖❖❖ **MC V AmEx DI DC**

Weinantz Food & Spirits

I-65 and State Road 46 West
Columbus, IN 47201
(812) 379-2323

For a truly Hoosier meal, Mayor Stewart recommends the Indiana-raised pork chop dinner at Weinantz. But, if you like steak, the meat is fresh and served to your liking. Other recommendations include the baby back ribs and beef liver with onions. Reservations accepted.

Open: 11 a.m.-2 p.m., 5 p.m.-9:30 p.m. M-F; 5-10 p.m. S, closed Su
Dress: casual ❖❖❖ **MC V AmEx DI DC**

ELLETTSVILLE

restaurant nominated by Diana K. Evans, clerk-treasurer

The Village Inn

309 East Temperance Street
Ellettsville, IN 47429
(812) 876-2204

On SR 46, across from the Ellettsville Police & Fire Station.

Stop by The Village Inn to enjoy great homestyle cooking and catch up on local and world events at the liars' bench. Clerk-Treasurer Evans recommends the fish sandwiches. On Thursdays, try the all-you-can-eat buffet. Reservations accepted.

Open: 6 a.m.-8 p.m. T-Su, closed Monday
Dress: very casual ❖

GREENSBURG

restaurants nominated by William H. Hunter, councilmember

While you're in Greensburg, don't miss the famous Tower Trees growing on the roof of the courthouse. They've been sighted there since 1870.

Cattlemen's Inn

1703 North Lincoln Street
Greensburg, IN 47240
(812) 663-2411

If it's steak or chicken you want, don't miss Cattlemen's Inn, where broasted chicken and ribeye steaks are the specialties of the house. Councilmember Hunter suggests that you try the broasted chicken special. Reservations accepted.
Open: 6 a.m.-8 p.m. T-Su, closed Monday
Dress: very casual   ❖

Mangs Family Restaurant & Bakery

I-74 and State Road 3
335 Smith Road
Greensburg, IN 47240
(812) 663-4633

I-74 & State Road 3

Any time of day, Mangs will satisfy your appetite with an array of mouth watering items from reuben sandwiches to chicken alfredo. Wednesdays feature International Night highlighting different ethnic foods each week. Virtually all breakfast, lunch and dinner items are available any time of day. Reservations accepted.
Open: 24-hours daily, closed Christmas day
Dress: casual   ❖❖   MC V AmEx Di

Storie's Restaurant

109 East Main Street
Greensburg, IN 47240
(812) 663-9948

After you've looked at the famous Tower Trees growing on the roof of the Greensburg courthouse, cross the street to Storie's, where you can enjoy delicious fried chicken, fresh-cut breaded pork tenderloins and mouth watering homemade pies. Sorry, no reservations.
Open: 8:30 a.m.-7:30 p.m. M-S, closed Su
Dress: casual   ❖

LAWRENCEBURG

restaurants nominated by Donald Combs, mayor;
Deborah Rainey, clerk-treasurer, Greendale

Karp's Kafe

232 West High Street
Lawrenceburg, IN 47025
(812) 537-3180

Located on the first floor of a three-story antique mall in downtown Lawrenceburg, Karp's is a perfect rest stop for the weary shopper. Mayor Combs suggests the reuben sandwich and the grilled chicken salad. Sorry, no reservations.
Open: 11 a.m.-3:30 p.m. Su-F, closed S
Dress: very casual   ❖

Whiskey's Historic Family Restaurant

334 Front Street
Lawrenceburg, IN 47025
(812) 537-4239

Located on U.S. 50 west, 3 lights from I-275.

And what else would you name a restaurant located in a city that boasts two of the nation's largest distilleries: Seagram's and Schenley. After you work up an appetite by touring the distilleries, Greendale Clerk-Treasurer Rainey suggests you try the delicious cod fish dinner after savoring the barbecued potato skins as an appetizer. The smoked ribs and steaks are good, too. Reservations accepted.
Open: 11:30 a.m.-10 p.m. M-Th, 11:30 a.m.-11 p.m. F,
5 p.m.-11 p.m. S, closed Su
Dress: casual   ❖❖❖   **MC V AmEx Di**

SOUTH CENTRAL

Did you know?
Vernon is the only town deviating from the November election. Under the state charter of 1851, voting is to be conducted on the first Monday in March. Vernon also is the only town in Indiana with a mayor.

LINTON

The Dutch Oven

90 North East A Street
Linton, IN 47441
(812) 847-4581

One block east of the intersection of state roads 54 and 59, across from Wolf's City Service and NAPA.

The Dutch Oven features the largest buffet and salad bar in the area, plus a dazzling list of other breakfast, lunch and dinner menu items. Popular selections include ham and cheese sandwiches and beef Manhattans. The steaks and prime rib aren't bad, either. Don't miss one of their tantalizing fresh desserts. Reservations accepted.

**Open: 5 a.m.-2 p.m. M, 5 a.m.-8 p.m. T-Th, 5 a.m.-9 p.m. F-Su
Dress: casual**   ❖❖

The Grill

60 A Street North East
Linton, IN 47441
(812) 847-9010

You're in coal mining country when you're in Linton. You'll enjoy learning about the area's rich mining heritage by browsing around the interior of The Grill. Take a good look at the display of coal mining photographs. If you have a miner's appetite, try the tenderloin and fries. Breakfast is served anytime. Sorry, no reservations.

**Open: 5 a.m.-6 p.m. M-Th, 5 a.m.-8 p.m. F-S, 5 a.m.-2 p.m. Su
Dress: very casual**   ❖❖

restaurant nominated by Lana Lynn, clerk-treasurer, Dugger

Stoll's Country Inn

Highway 54
Linton, IN 47441
(812) 847-2477

Dugger Clerk-Treasurer Lynn likes to travel to Linton to savor the Amish atmosphere and food of Stoll's. Every dish is made from scratch at this friendly establishment. Sorry, no reservations.

**Open: 7 a.m.-8 p.m. M-Th, 7 a.m.-9 p.m. F-S, closed Su
Dress: casual**

LOOGOOTEE

restaurant nominated by William Parker, mayor

Stoll's Lakeview Restaurant

Highway 231 North
Loogootee, IN 47553
(812) 295-3299

Relax in the old-world charm of the Amish at Stoll's Lakeview Restaurant. A large open buffet features Amish style food. Try the fried chicken or roast beef and noodles. The dressing and bread pudding complement any meal. Reservations accepted.
Open: 6 a.m.-9 p.m. M-S, closed Su
Dress: casual   ❖❖   **MC V Di**

MADISON

Hammon's Restaurant

221 East Main
Madison, IN 47250
(812) 265-3237

Its hometown atmosphere makes Hammon's a popular local meeting place for folks in Madison. You'll find the menu full of fresh meats and vegetables. There are a variety of homemade pies, made daily. Sorry, no reservations.
Open: 5 a.m.-4 p.m. M-S, closed Su
Dress: very casual   ❖

Upper Crust

209 West Main Street
Madison, IN 47250
(812) 265-6727

Chef Nick Izamis tempts your tastebuds with unique European cuisine at Upper Crust. Located in the heart of Madison's historic district, the restaurant features daily chef's specials with fresh breads. Be sure to try the Greek salad. Reservations advised.
Open: 11 a.m.-2 p.m. M-S, 5-9 p.m. M-Th, 5-10 p.m. F-S, closed Su
Dress: casual/dressy   ❖❖❖   **MC V**

Did you know?
The oldest volunteer fire company in Indiana is The Fair Play Company No. 1, a fire station at Madison.

SOUTH CENTRAL

Zepplin's Deli

719 West Main Street
Madison, IN 47250
(812) 265-DELI

A unique deli located in a historic trolley barn in downtown Madison, Zepplin's will pique your interest by it's unusually named sandwiches alone. Offerings include the Lead Zepplin, a 12-inch meat sandwich, and the Un-leaded Zepplin, a veggie sandwich. Sorry, no reservations.
Open: 10 a.m.-7 p.m. M-S, closed Su
Dress: very casual   ◆◆

METAMORA
restaurant nominated by Alberta Sauerland, clerk-treasurer, Brookville

Hearthstone Restaurant

18149 U.S. 52
Metamora, IN 47030
(317) 647-5204

Located near beautiful, historic Metamora, one of the few canal era "boom towns," the Hearthstone is declared by Brookville Clerk-Treasurer Sauerland to have "one of the best salad bars around." Her favorite is the pan fried chicken. If surroundings look familiar, it's because scenes from the 1988 hit movie *Rainman* were shot here. Reservations accepted.
Open: 10 a.m.-9 p.m. T-F, 10 a.m.-10 p.m. S, 10 a.m.-8 p.m. Su
Dress: casual   ◆◆   **MC V DI**

MILAN

Milan Railroad Inn

East Carr Street
Milan, IN 47031
(812) 654-2800 or 1-800-448-7405

If you enjoyed the movie *Hoosiers*, you'll delight in the memorabilia of the 1954 Milan High School State Basketball Champions proudly displayed on the walls of the Railroad Inn. You'll find delicious Indiana fried chicken, steaks, chops, seafood, and an unusual soup and salad bar. Reservations accepted.
Open: 11 a.m.-8 p.m. M-F, 11 a.m.-9 p.m. S-Su
Dress: casual   ◆◆/◆◆◆   **MC V**

The Reservation

1001 Warpath Drive
Milan, IN 47031
(812) 654-2224

Take Exit 156 off I-74, go south on SR 101 about 11 miles to Milan.

Besides being home of the 1954 state basketball champions, Milan also boasts some restaurants that are real winners. Among them is The Reservation, where you can enjoy hickory smoked barbecue country ribs on Thursdays and fried chicken or fish on Fridays, along with other daily specials. Reservations accepted.
Open: 5 a.m.-9 p.m. M-Th, 5 a.m.-10 p.m. F-S, 6 a.m.-9 p.m. Su
Dress: very casual ❖

Villa Milan Vineyard

County Road 50 North
Milan, IN 47031
(812) 654-3419

Italian entrees at Villa Milan are complemented by estate bottled wine. After attending a free wine tasting, enjoy your meal on the gazebo. Each Saturday evening from June-September, enjoy a hog roast dinner (reservations required). Be sure to purchase several bottles of your favorite Villa Milan wine before you leave—you won't find it anywhere else. Reservations accepted.
Open: 9 a.m.-8 p.m. M-S, closed Su
Dress: casual ❖❖ **MC V Di**

MONTGOMERY

The Gasthof Amish Restaurant and Village
★ See Top Ten list, page 3 ★

NORTH VERNON

restaurant nominated by John G. Hall, mayor

Broad Acres

Route 5
North Vernon, IN 47265
(812) 346-2773

Located on SR 7, 3 miles north of North Vernon.

Mayor Hall especially likes to hold small luncheon meetings at Broad Acres, where his favorite dish is the roast beef and mashed potato dinner. He confesses to being a frequent visitor to the buffet table, too. Reservations accepted.
Open: 11 a.m.-9 p.m. T-F, 7:30 a.m.-9 p.m. S, 7:30 a.m.-6 p.m. Su, closed M
Dress: very casual ❖❖ **MC V**

OLDENBURG

restaurant nominated by Mary Jo Dietz, clerk-treasurer

Brau Haus

Wasserstrasse
Oldenburg, IN 47036
(812) 934-4840

Look for the church and convent towers looming above the hilltops of this German-settled "Town of Spires" and watch for the huge mural on the west wall of the Brau Haus, next to the parking lot. The fried chicken and salad bar are superb, according to Clerk-Treasurer Dietz, and well worth the drive. German beers, reasonable prices and a friendly atmosphere are enticements at the Brau Haus. Reservations accepted.

**Open: 10 a.m.-10 p.m. M-F, 10 a.m.-11 p.m. S,
11 a.m.-8 p.m. Su**
Dress: very casual   ❖❖   **MC V AmEx**

Wagner's Village Inn

Main Street
Oldenburg, IN 47036
(812) 934-3854

Don't be fooled by the tavern-like facade; Wagner's is a large, family-oriented tavern-restaurant with friendly and fast service. Try to spend two days in Oldenburg if only to savor the fried chicken at both Wagner's and Brau Haus and then try to decide which is better. Local folks have been trying to decide for years. Steaks and seafood also are available. Reservations accepted.

**Open: 10 a.m.-9 p.m. T-Th, 10 a.m.-10 p.m. F, 11 a.m.-10 p.m. S,
11 a.m.-8 p.m. Su, closed M**
Dress: casual   ❖❖   **MC V**

RISING SUN

restaurant nominated by Mark A. Guard, mayor

Tom & Jerry's Sports Bar

143 Main Street
Rising Sun, IN 47040
(812) 438-4600

If you're an I.U. fan, you won't want to miss Tom & Jerry's Sports Bar where the decor has a distinctly Hoosier flavor. Even if you aren't a sports fan, though, you'll still enjoy the delicious food. Mayor Guard suggests the barbecued chicken, but all of

the large sandwiches are tasty. Also popular are the fried cod
dinner and the chili. Reservations accepted.
Open: 9 a.m.-midnight M-S, 11 a.m.-midnight Su
Dress: very casual   ❖

SEYMOUR

restaurant nominated by John Burkhart, mayor

Gerth Cafe

119 East Second Street
Seymour, IN 47274
(812) 522-5523

Open 365 days a year, the Gerth Cafe has been a local favorite
for over 60 years. Mayor Burkhart recommends the tenderloin,
white beans and fried potatoes. Sorry, no reservations.
Open: 5 a.m.-11 p.m. daily
Dress: casual   ❖

STORY

The Story Inn
★ See Top Ten list, page 2 ★

VERNON

Robert's Pike Street Restaurant

14 Pike Street
Vernon, IN 47282
(812) 346-1390

A refreshingly different kind of restaurant in a historic 1800s
downtown Vernon building, Robert's Pike Street Restaurant offers
a warm and cheerful interior reflecting the era of the building.
Try the all-you-can-eat Alaskan whitefish dinner or the outstanding pizza. Reservations accepted.
Open: 11 a.m.-2 p.m., 5-9 p.m. daily
Dress: casual   ❖

*From state
roads 3 and 7
turn on Pike St.,
it's across from
the Courthouse.*

SOUTH CENTRAL

Did you know?
The only city in the United States to have a
continuous annual observance for veterans
since World War II is Seymour, which has had
a V-J Day parade each August since 1945.

VEVAY

Located on SR 56 across the street from Switzerland County High School.

The Ogle Haus

1013 West Main Street
Vevay, IN 47043
(812) 427-2020

Fine dining and a breathtaking view of the beautiful Ohio River makes the Ogle Haus a unique establishment among locals in this Swiss-settled community. After a tour of the town, including the birthplace of Edward Eggleston, author of *The Hoosier School Master,* try a local favorite at The Ogle Haus, the grilled chicken with fresh fruit. Sorry, no reservations.

Open: 7 a.m.-8 p.m. Su-Th, 7 a.m.-9 p.m. F-S
Dress: casual ◆◆◆ **MC V AmEx CB Di DC**

VINCENNES

Charlie's Smorgasbord

1027 Washington Avenue
Vincennes, IN 47591
(812) 882-5115

Entrees change daily at Charlie's Smorgasboard, where you can choose from four meat selections. The local favorites are the pork chops and fried chicken. Watch for the restaurant to relocate to Kimmel Road between U.S. 41 and Hart Street in September 1995. Reservations accepted for banquet facility only.

Open: 10:30 a.m.-8 p.m. Su-Th, 10:30-9 p.m. F-S
Dress: casual ◆ **MC V**

Market Street Restaurant & Pub

106 St. Honory Place
Vincennes, IN 47592
(812) 886-5201

The Market Street Restaurant & Pub boasts "the best barbecue ribs in town," and a delicious array of steaks, seafood and pasta in an antique-filled atmosphere. Be sure to check out the tea pot room. Reservations accepted.

Open: 11 a.m.-9:30 p.m. M-Th, 11 a.m.-10:30 p.m. F,
noon-10:30 p.m. S, closed Su
Dress: casual ◆◆/◆◆◆ **MC V AmEx DI DC**

WASHINGTON

restaurant nominated by Tom Baumert, mayor

The Washington Steamer

21 East Main Street
Washington, IN 47501
(812) 254-9973

While walking down Main Street in Washington, just follow the aroma of onions being cooked and you'll discover the best hamburgers with grilled onions in town, according to Mayor Baumert. They're easy to spot, too, according to the mayor because you can view the hamburgers being cooked through the front window of the steamer. Sorry, no reservations.

Open: 5 a.m.-6 p.m. M-Th, S; 5 a.m.-7 p.m. F, closed Su
Dress: casual

WHEATLAND

restaurant nominated by Millicent P. Watson, clerk-treasurer;
Katherine Turner, councilmember

J.D.'s Fountain

North Broadway
State Road 550
Wheatland, IN 47597
(812) 321-5800

Enjoy an old-fashioned malt, float, sundae, or a flavored Coke (with ice shaved from a block!) at J.D.'s Fountain. Actor Alvy Moore (Mr. Kimball of *Green Acres*) stops in for his favorite—a chocolate Coke—when he's in town. Clerk-Treasurer Watson also recommends you try the chili, pizza and hand-dipped ice cream. Sorry, no reservations.

Open: 8 a.m.-8 p.m. M-T, Th-S, 8 a.m.-6 p.m. W, closed Su
Dress: very casual ❖

Did you know?
Between 1800 and 1813, Vincennes served as the Indiana Territory capitol under Gov. William Henry Harrison.

SOUTH CENTRAL

Like what you've seen?

> ## Prices per copy
> 1- 24 copy(ies) $9.95
> 25-49 copies $7.50
> 50-149 copies $6.95
> over 150 copies $6
> prices do not include shipping and handling

---

name   title

---

address   municipality   zip

---

phone (area code)   fax

❑ Enclosed is my check/claim form (make payable to IACT).

❑ Please invoice me ($5 processing fee on all invoice orders).

● **Sales Tax**: Purchase for personal use must include sales tax. Purchase by non-profit group or municipality does not require sales tax payment, but must include exempt number in box below.

qty	title	unit price	subtotal
	Indiana's Favorite Hometown Restaurants		
		5% IN sales tax ●	
		shipping/handling	
		invoice fee	
		Total	

Shipping/handling charges (if delivery is required)

1 book .... add $1.75
2-9 .... add $2.75
10-25 .... add $5.75
26-50 .... add $7.75
over 50 .... add $10

> ● ❑ I've not included sales tax in my order, and here is my tax exempt number for your records.
>
> _____

Your copy(ies) will be shipped within 5 working days of receipt. Please fax or mail your response to: *Indiana's Favorite Hometown Restaurants*, **150 West Market Street, Suite 728, Indianapolis, IN 46204 or fax to (317) 237-6206.**

Treat yourself to the rolling hills of Southern Indiana

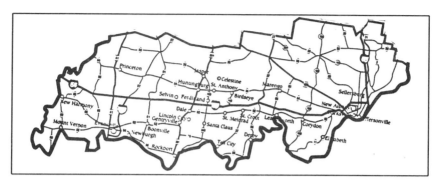

Just above the majestic Ohio River lies Southern Indiana, a land that gets its shape from the river, its terrain from the glaciers and its personality from the people. In Southern Indiana, the boyhood residence of Abraham Lincoln, you'll find the state's first capitol and the nation's first theme park...breathtaking cathedrals and vintage baseball diamonds...ancient fossils and virgin timber...cool caves and spicy barbecue.

A few notable natives of this area include New York Yankees first baseman Don Mattingly (Evansville), Boston Celtic great Larry Bird (French Lick), baseball hall-of-famer Ed Roush (Oakland City), and Brady Bunch mom Florence Henderson (Dale).

In this magical region—outlined by the Wabash and Ohio rivers and rippling with flowered hillsides, golden raintrees and pristine old German settlements—you'll find a variety of dream getaways.

In Jeffersonville, start your trip in the 119-building riverfront historic district and the Howard Steamboat Museum.

Next stop is Scottsburg's historic town square and the two-level Scottsburg Antique Mall, both worth a browse.

Take the backroads to Huntingburg, where you'll find hundreds of restored instruments at Dr. Ted's Musical Marvels, a turn-of-the-century musical tour. Huntingburg also is home to League Stadium, one of the two baseball diamonds featured in *A League of Their Own*. In Jasper, take the walking tour and visit St. Joseph's Church with its outstanding Romanesque architecture and Austrian mosaics. For a game of golf, try Sultan's Run Golf Course, ranked in the state's top five.

Strange-but-true, you'll find a one-of-a-kind Mortician's Museum in Boonville, along with the beautiful Scales Lake Park.

In Tell City, stop off at the Tell City Pretzel Company. The 140-year-old company still makes its pretzels the

old-fashioned way, by hand twisting. The 20-minute tour concludes with a free pretzel. The Falls of the Ohio near Clarksville is where the world's largest exposed fossil bed, once a coral reef, is located. In New Albany, the Culbertson Mansion Historic Site is a place to see. This 25-room, three-story estate of William Culbertson, one of Indiana's wealthiest men, was built in 1867 and boasts hand-painted ceilings, a carved rosewood staircase and marble chandeliers.

Newburgh offers guided tours to the many beautifully restored buildings located there. Country store buffs should visit the Newburgh Country Store, complete with a cracker barrel, potbellied stove and a player piano.

From there, travel to Evansville where such places as the historic Angel Mounds are located. One of the best preserved prehistoric Indian settlements in the U.S., Angel Mounds includes reconstructed homes, round houses, a temple and a stockade wall. Burdette

Park in Evansville is the largest water park in Southern Indiana. On its 145 acres you'll find an Olympic-size swimming pool with four water slides, batting cages, miniature golf, camping, cabins, hiking trails, and bike paths. And don't forget to take in the wild things at Mesker Park Zoo. At 67 acres, it's Indiana's largest zoo and home to nearly 700 animals from around the world.

No trip would be complete without a stop at New Harmony, an enchanting community nationally recognized for its historic preservation, contemporary architecture and two attempts to create a utopian society in the 1800s. Also, the Labyrinth will help you contemplate life's mysterious paths as you wind your way through a European hedge-maze. In the center lies the House of Meditation.

These are but a few of the adventures that await you in Southern Indiana. For more information, contact the local visitors bureaus listed below:

Dubois County.........(812) 282-9115 or 1-800-ADVENTURE

Evansville...................(812) 425-5402 or 1-800-433-3025

Historic Southern Indiana (New Harmony).....................

....(812) 465-7014

Perry County...(812) 547-2385

Warrick County.......................................(812) 897-2340

BOONVILLE

restaurants nominated by Jack Schreve, councilmember

Locust Street Cafe

118 West Locust Street
Boonville, IN 47601
(812) 897-4724

Head for the south side of town square, the cafe is across from the courthouse.

The Locust Street Cafe on the south side of the city square is open for lunch only. The daily lunch special and the homemade desserts are something you won't want to miss. Desserts are made fresh daily. Reservations accepted.

Open: 11 a.m.-2 p.m. M-F, closed S-Su
Dress: casual   ❖   **MC V**

Lee's Garden Chinese Restaurant

966 West Main Street
Boonville, IN 47601
(812) 897-5420

If Chinese food is what you crave, relax amid the red and gold tones of Lee's Garden where the lunch buffet is a must-try. Visitors give high ratings to the Hunan combination and the oriental chicken, too. Reservations accepted.

Open: 11 a.m.-2 p.m. M, 11 a.m.-9 p.m. T-Th, 11 a.m.-10 p.m. F-S, 11 a..m.-9 p.m. Su
Dress: casual   ❖❖   **MC V AmEx DI**

BORDEN

restaurants nominated by Ruth Sparks, clerk-treasurer

Joe Huber Family Restaurant

2421 Scottsville Road
Borden, IN 47106
(812) 923-5255

Take Exit 1 off I-265 on to State St., at Floyds Knobs go north on Scottsville Rd.

Enjoy the rolling hills of Southern Indiana at Joe Huber Family Farm, Orchard and Restaurant. For a satisfying meal, try the Huber Country Platter dinner served family style, featuring fresh vegetables and their famous fried biscuits. After dinner, if you have room, taste one of their fabulous home-cooked desserts. Reservations accepted.

Open: 11 a.m.-8 p.m. M-Th, 11 a.m.-9 p.m. F-S, 11 a.m.-6 p.m. Su, May-October; closed M-Th November-April
Dress: casual   ❖❖❖

SOUTHERN

Stumler's Restaurant & Orchard

10924 St. Johns Road
Borden, IN 47106

Give your tastebuds a treat with delicious farm fresh food at
Stumler's Restaurant & Orchard. Relax in the country-fresh air
while you enjoy fried chicken, country ham, and stir-fry chicken,
or try the roast beef buffet. Fresh vegetables from the farm are
served in season. Reservations accepted.
Open: daily
Dress: casual   ❖❖/❖❖❖   **MC V AmEx**

DALE

Windell's Cafe

Hwy. 62 East, P.O. Box 491
Dale, IN 47523
(812) 937-4253

*Windell's is at
the junction of
U.S. 231 and SR
62.*

Since 1947 diners have enjoyed the fare at Windell's Cafe,
dubbed "The Eating Place of Mid-America's Crossroads." Tempt
your tastebuds with their homemade chicken and dumplings or
ribs and sauerkraut. And top it off with a piece of mouth-
watering homemade pie for dessert. Reservations accepted.
Open: 5 a.m.-8 p.m. Su-F, 5:30 a.m.-9 p.m. S
Dress: very casual   ❖

Colonial Cafeteria

Hwy 231 South
P.O. Box 468
Dale, IN 47523
(812) 937-2330

*Colonial Cafeteria
is just 2 miles
south of I-64 on
U.S. 231.*

Regulars at Colonial Cafeteria will tell you that this is where you
get your money's worth if you're looking for good home-cooked
food. Favorites include broasted chicken and meat loaf, along
with cooked cabbage, pinto beans and many other fresh
vegetable selections. The list of homemade pies is endless:
pecan, custard, pumpkin, apple, berry.... Reservations accepted.
Open: 5 a.m.-6 p.m., daily
Dress: very casual   ❖

> *Did you know?*
> At 67 acres, Mesker Park Zoo in Evansville is
> the state's largest zoo.

Johnson's Pizza Plus Barbecue

12 South Washington (Hwy. 231)
P.O. Box 346
Dale, IN 47523
(812) 937-4431

Johnson's Pizza Plus Barbecue serves up delicious barbecue and
excellent pizza at reasonable prices. The barbecue buffet is
extraordinary. Try the barbecue specials from 4-7:30 p.m.
Wednesdays and noon-7:30 p.m. Saturdays. And leave room
for something from their ice cream shop! Reservations accepted.
Open: 11 a.m.-10 p.m. Su-Th, 11 a.m.-midnight F-S
Dress: casual   ❖

EVANSVILLE

Hilltop Inn

1100 Harmony Way
Evansville, IN 47712
(812) 422-1757

The Hilltop Inn is a historic treasure as well as a popular local
eatery. Established in 1839 as a stagecoach depot, the Hilltop
Inn now treats travelers to fine southwestern cuisine, including
excellent fish platters and sandwiches. Popular local favorites are
brain sandwiches and fiddlers. Located on the hilly west side
near the Evansville Zoo, the Hilltop Inn is sure to satisfy your
cravings. Reservations advised.
Open: 9 a.m.-midnight M-S, closed Su.
Dress: very casual   ❖❖   **MC V**

*Take Lloyd Expy.
west to St.
Joseph Ave.; right
on St. Joseph to
Maryland St. (3rd
stoplight); left on
Maryland to the
"top of the hill."*

Mattingly's 23

1700 Morgan Center Drive
Evansville, IN 47715
(812) 473-4323

If you're a hungry baseball fan, you'll hit a home run at this
restaurant owned by New York Yankees great Don Mattingly.
Enjoy the sports memorabilia filling the dining area, or challenge a
friend to a game of basketball "horse" to work up an appetite.
And, when you do so, the recommendation at Mattingly's is the
hearty hamburgers. Reservations accepted.
Open: 11 a.m.-midnight M-F, 11 a.m.-1 a.m. F-S, closed Su
Dress: casual   ❖❖/❖❖❖ **MC V AmEx CB DI DC**

*Mattingly's decor
features an
authentic Yankee
Stadium bar and
a complete
hardwood floor
dining area.*

FERDINAND

restaurants nominated by Charles Schuler, councilmember

Fleigs Cafe

905 Main Street
Ferdinand, IN 47532
(812) 367-1310

Take Exit 63 off I-64, go 1/2 mile north to 9th and Main.

Town Councilmember Schuler raves about the friendly small-town atmosphere and the excellent food at Fleigs Cafe. He rates the chicken and pan fried steak as "awesome." The fiddlers are popular, too. Reservations accepted.
Open: 7 a.m.-midnight M-S, closed Su
Dress: very casual   ❖❖

The Covered Bridge

835 Main Street
Ferdinand, IN 47532
(812) 367-1501

Relax and enjoy the atmosphere at The Covered Bridge, Ferdinand's oldest cafe/tavern, where diners have enjoyed home-cooked meals since 1930. Sorry, no reservations.
Open: 7:30 a..m.-midnight M-S, closed Su
Dress: very casual   ❖

Ferdy Flyer

133 West 10th Street
Ferdinand, IN 47523
(812) 367-2222

As the name suggests, fast service is the specialty at Ferdy Flyer, along with a heaping serving of Hoosier hospitality, according to Councilmember Schuler. The restaurant was named after the Ferdy Flyer Railroad which served Ferdinand some years ago. Just five miles long, it was the shortest railroad in the state. A sign on the roof of the restaurant is a replica of the Ferdy Flyer train. Reservations advised.
Open: 8 a.m.-10 p.m. daily
Dress: casual   ❖

Did you know?
The first civil settlement in the Northwest Territory in what became Indiana was Clarksville. It became the state's first incorporated town. The town book was begun in 1784.

Homestead Pizza

1510 Main Street
Ferdinand, IN 47532
(812) 367-1808

If you love the delicious taste of mouth watering pizza, Clerk-Treasurer Schulthise recommends Homestead Pizza. Try the restaurant's namesake Homestead Pizza (a loaded concoction) or their stromboli. Reservations accepted.

Open: 11 a.m.-10 p.m. Su-Th, 11 a.m.-midnight F-S
Dress: very casual ❖

HUNTINGBURG

restaurants nominated by Connie Nass, mayor

Fat & Sassy

403 North Jackson
Huntingburg, IN 47542
(812) 683-4801

Fat and Sassy's serves up delicious soups, salads and sandwiches. Mayor Nass recommends the Spring Salad. Soups are served in bread bowls, and Wednesday's feature is fresh-baked bread pudding. Also, try the large variety of flavored coffees and teas, or a treat from the only espresso/cappuccino machine in Dubois County. Sorry, no reservations.

Open: 11 a.m.-5:30 p.m. M-F, 10:30 a.m.-4 p.m. S, closed Su
Dress: casual ❖ MC V

Fourth Street Deli

304 Fourth Street
Huntingburg, IN 47542
(812) 683-5650

Take U.S. 231 north to Fourth St., go west 1 block (on right).

Home of the "Dubois Dookey," Fourth Street Deli offers visitors old-time deli decor and sumptuous deli sandwiches. The Dookey, a Southern Indiana classic, is served warm with roast beef, ham, turkey, lettuce, and a special sauce. The open-faced reuben sandwich is a popular favorite, along with the lemon chicken rice soup. Reservations accepted.

Open: 9 a.m.-3 p.m. M-S, closed Su
Dress: casual ❖ MC V

SOUTHERN

IRELAND

The Chicken Place

P.O. Box 134
Ireland, IN 47545
(812) 482-7600

From Jasper, take SR 56 west about 3 miles to Ireland.

For some out-of-this-world fried chicken, be sure to visit The Chicken Place. Regulars rave about the delicious German fries, too. Diners include Huntingburg Mayor Connie Nass, Jasper Mayor Bill Schmitt, and Little Jimmy Dickens. Reservations are accepted Monday-Thursday only.

Open: 4:30-9 p.m. M-F, 3:30-9 p.m. S, closed Su and holidays
Dress: very casual　　　　　❖❖　　　　　**MC V**

JASPER

restaurant nominated by Grayson Goodness, councilmember

Schnitzelbank

393 Third Avenue (Hwy. 162 S)
Jasper, IN 47546
(812) 482-2640

Be sure to sample the Gewürztraminer (a white wine produced and bottled in Indiana) or Schnitzelbank Weiss (a German wheat beer).

German food at its very best, along with charbroiled steaks, draw local diners as well as visitors from far away to this Jasper institution. The German decor provides an atmosphere which adds to the delight of diners, according to Councilmember Goodness. A gift shop provides an opportunity for guests to purchase some of the fine Southern Indiana wines and other products served at this favorite hometown restaurant.

Open: 8 a.m.-10 p.m. M-S, closed Su
Dress: casual　　　　　❖❖/❖❖❖　　　　　**MC V DI**

restaurant nominated by Bill Schmitt, mayor

Fiesta

1340 Mill Street
Jasper, IN 47547

For 48 years, the Fiesta restaurant has delighted diners with a variety of dishes from pizza to charbroiled steaks. Regulars rave about the German tenderloin and onion rings, and the barbecue is a popular selection as well. Sorry, no reservations.

Open: 11 a.m.-10 p.m. M-S, 4 p.m.-9 p.m. Su
Dress: casual　　　　　❖❖　　　　　**MC**

JEFFERSONVILLE

restaurants nominated by Donna Frantz, councilmember

Schimpff's Confectionery

347 Spring Street
Jeffersonville, IN 47130
(812) 283-8367

Councilmember Frantz praises the old-fashioned sandwiches and specialty desserts in the historic downtown confectionery. Because Schimpff's is one of the oldest candymakers in the Hoosier state, you have an obligation after eating to savor the delights at the antique soda fountain. No one can leave without purchasing some of their famous homemade candy. Warning: The Red Hots are just that—red hot. Sorry, no reservations.

Confectionery open: 10 a.m.-5 p.m. M-F, 10 a.m.-3 p.m. S
Lunch served: 11 a.m.-2 p.m. M-S, closed Su
Dress: very casual ❖ **MC V**

From I-65, take SR 62 Exit to Charlestown. Turn right at the first stoplight (Spring St.), and go about 6 blocks.

MILLTOWN

restaurants nominated by Lula M. Combs, clerk-treasurer;
William Dubois, councilmember; W. Rusk Roggenkamp, councilmember

Blue River Cafe

128 West Main Street
Milltown, IN 47145
(812) 633-7510

Located in the oldest building in this small town once famous for its mill and limestone kilns, the Blue River Cafe has the unanimous endorsement of the town's elected leaders, who favor the relaxing atmosphere. Their recommendations include the white chili, orange roughy and vegetarian entrees. Reservations advised.

Open: 11 a.m.-9 p.m. F-S, 11 a.m.-3 p.m. Su, closed M-Th
Dress: casual ❖❖ **MC V**

Blue River Cafe is one mile off SR 64, at the corner of First and Main.

SOUTHERN

Did you know?
The nation's largest inland shipyard is Jeffboat, Inc., located at Jeffersonville. The company has launched over 6,200 vessels since it was founded in 1938.

MOUNT VERNON
restaurant nominated by Jackson Higgins, mayor

Gundi's Restaurant

132 East Second Street
Mount Vernon, IN 47620
(812) 838-4661

Gundi's is 2 blocks north of SR 62 at Second and Walnut, by the 119-year-old Posey County Courthouse.

Mayor Higgins says Gundi's is *the* place for family dining in Mount Vernon—the state's southwesternmost city and home to the thriving Southwind Maritime Centre. The mayor is especially fond of the bratwurst and sauerkraut, and heartily recommends the homemade rhubarb pie. Among the 10 daily plate lunches, local favorites include the chicken and dumplings and the stuffed breaded tenderloins. This favorite meeting site for local business leaders and civic clubs also plates predawn barge-sized breakfasts. Reservations advised on weekends.

Open: 4:30 a.m.-8 p.m. M-S, 5:30 a.m.-7 p.m. Su
Dress: casual   ◆◆   **MC V DI**

NEW HARMONY
restaurants nominated by Gary Watson, councilmember

The Bayou Grill Restaurant

600 North Street
New Harmony, IN 47631
(812) 682-4431

30 minutes west of Evansville on SR 66, turn right at the light, go 2 blocks, and turn right again.

Beautiful gardens surround The Bayou Grill, and the atmosphere inside is equally enjoyable with many fine original works of art on display. Enjoy their fabulous Sunday Brunch where you'll be tempted with Belgian waffles, omelettes made to order, fresh fruits, salads, and a vast array of pastries and desserts. The Bayou also offers a scrumptious buffet on Friday and Saturday nights. Reservations advised.

Open: 7 a.m.-8 p.m. Su-Th, 7 a.m.-9 p.m. F-S
Dress: casual   ◆◆   **MC V AmEx DI**

> *Did you know?*
> The town of New Harmony is home to the first public school system.

SOUTHERN

The Red Geranium Restaurant

504 North Street
New Harmony, IN 47631
(812) 682-4431

Whether you're staying overnight in historic New Harmony, or just stopping by to eat, The Red Geranium in the New Harmony Inn is a delight. Meals are provided in a comfortable country inn atmosphere. Councilmember Watson recommends the char prime steak, spinach salad and Shaker lemon pie as dishes "you definitely must try." Reservations advised.

**Open: 11 a.m.-10 p.m. T-Th, 11 a.m.-11p.m. F-S,
11 a.m.-8 p.m. Su, closed M**
Dress: dressy ❖❖❖❖ MC V AmEx DI

NEWBURGH

The Landing Family Restaurant

2 East Water Street
Newburgh, IN 47630
(812) 858-2443

The Landing is located one block off the intersection of state roads 662 and 261—on the waterfront.

Not only is good food on the menu at the Landing, the restaurant feeds the soul with a panoramic view overlooking the Ohio River where you can watch magnificent sunsets, boat activity and barge traffic. Relax and enjoy such local favorites as ostrich burgers and reuben sandwiches. Reservations accepted.

**Open: 7 a.m.-9 p.m. T-Th, 7 a.m.-10 p.m. F-S, 7 a.m.-8 p.m. Su,
closed M (hours vary slightly in winter)**
Dress: casual ❖❖ MC V AmEx DI

restaurant nominated by John Hillenbrand, town manager, Chandler

The Old Homestead Inn

10233 State Road 662
Newburgh, IN 47630
(812) 853-3631

Large portions served family style are what appeals to Chandler Town Manager Hillenbrand at The Old Homestead Inn. His favorites are the chicken and roast beef, and the corn fritters with honey butter. Reservations accepted.

Open: 5-8 p.m. W-S, 11 a.m.-2 p.m. Su, closed M-T
Dress: casual ❖❖ MC V

OAKLAND CITY

restaurant nominated by Judy Cochrane, clerk-treasurer

Pipers Pizza House

Highway 57
Oakland City, IN 47660
(812) 749-4205

Located just 100 feet from Indiana's shortest state highway (SR 357), Pipers has a history of serving delicious meals—it began as a drive-in in the 1940s. Although pizza is the specialty of the house these days, you'll also find seven kinds of Italian sandwiches, chef and Greek salads, breadsticks and their private recipe spaghetti and meatballs. Reservations accepted.
Open: 10 a.m.-9 p.m. Su-Th, 10 a.m.-11 p.m. F-S
Dress: very casual   ❖

PEKIN

Nanny's Country Kitchen

P.O. Box 94
Pekin, IN 47165
(812) 967-4802

Nanny's is a home away from home for regulars—and visitors—who have time on their hands. Stop by the liars' table to catch up on the latest happenings, and see the "wall of fame," pictures of Nanny's regulars. Enjoy biscuits and gravy and home fried potatoes, or try one of the plate lunches. Reservations accepted.
Open: 5 a.m.-8 p.m. M-F, 5 a.m.-6 p.m. S, 6-10 a.m. Su
Dress: very casual   ❖

ROCKPORT

The Rockport Inn

Located 3 1/2 hours south of Indianapolis; 2 hours west of Louisville, KY; and 4 hours from St. Louis.

130 South Third Street
Rockport, IN 47635
(812) 649-2664

While at the Rockport Inn, keep your eyes open for the resident ghost. After all, the inn has been in operation since 1857. Whether you're staying overnight, or just for dinner, be sure to try the surf and turf or prime rib. After dinner, select your dessert from a list of fresh inn-made pies. Reservations advised.
Open: 5-9 p.m. M-S, 11a.m.-3 p.m. Su
Dress: casual   ❖❖❖   **MC V**

The Rockport Junction

Junction of 231, 66 and 45
(812) 649-2700

Reasonable prices for great home-cooked food is the lure of the
Rockport Junction, located at the junction of scenic Indiana
highways 231, 66 and 45. Local folks praise the salad and
food bar, and kids love the caboose (yes, you can dine inside!).
On Fridays, try the fiddlers; Saturdays feature barbecue. Sorry,
no reservations.
Open: 10 a.m.-8 p.m. Su-Th, 10 a.m.-9 p.m. F-S
Dress: casual ❖

SCOTTSBURG

restaurant nominated by Stanley Tucker, councilmember, Sellersburg

Company's Coming

64 South Main Street
Scottsburg, IN 47170
(812) 752-6559

*Exit I-65 at
SR 56, go
east 1 mile, the
restaurant is
on the west
side of the
courthouse
square.*

A relaxed and friendly ambience awaits you at Company's
Coming on the courthouse square in Scottsburg. Located in a
turn-of-the-century building, it's a true find. Browse in the gift
area or treat yourself to great chocolates and candies. The lunch
and dinner menus will delight any palate—from hometown
Mayor Bill Graham's favorite dish, steak au poivre, to their
famous "soup in a bread bowl." Sellersburg Councilmember
Tucker rates the food as "outstanding!" Reservations advised.
**Open: 9 a.m.-5 p.m. M, 9 a.m.-8 p.m. T-Th, 9 a.m.-9 p.m. F-S,
11 a.m.-3 p.m. S**
Dress: casual ❖❖❖ **MC V AmEx**

Did you know?
The first city in the nation to discontinue
garbage collection and install waste disposers in each house was Jasper, on August 1,
1950. The reduction in taxes was expected
to help pay for the costs of the disposers.

SELLERSBURG

Neil's Place

7611 Highway 311
Sellersburg, IN 47172

Owned by the local Smith family for about 30 years, Neil's is considered the number one restaurant in Sellersburg. The favorite dishes of local officials include the onion soup, fish sandwiches and the garlic toast with apple butter. Reservations accepted.

Open: 11 a.m.-11 p.m. M-S, 11 a.m.-9 p.m. Su
Dress: casual   ◆◆   MC V AmEx

WARRENTON

The Log Inn
★ See Top Ten list, page 2 ★

Index

Cities/Towns

*=unincorporated communities